Pools of Fresh Water

Pools of Fresh Water

Frances Parsons

TRiANGLE

First published 1987
Triangle
SPCK
Holy Trinity Church
Marylebone Road
London NW1 4DU

British Library Cataloguing in Publication Data

Parsons, Frances
  Pools of fresh water.
  1. Rheumatoid arthritis—Patients—
  Biography
  I. Title
  362.1'96722'00924 3   RC933

ISBN 0–281–04287–X

Photoset by Inforum Ltd, Portsmouth.
Printed in Great Britain by
Hazell, Watson & Viney Limited
Member of the BPCC Group
Aylesbury, Bucks

For Stephen, Anna and Clare

Acknowledgements

I owe the existence of this book mainly to my husband, Stephen. He has encouraged, coaxed, typed, corrected and retyped, and all with characteristic good humour.

I would also like to thank all those who have allowed me to use their stories and I must mention that, apart from those of my family and close friends, the names and some details of the characters have been changed in order to protect their identity.

Lastly I must thank my children, Anna and Clare, who have supported me by behaving as though authorship were a natural state and have never complained during the preparation of this manuscript.

Frances Parsons
Lugwardine
July 1986

It was 7.30 on a Wednesday morning in February when the bedroom door opened and a little person peered round, pottered across the room, climbed over the sleeping forms and snuggled down into bed between her parents. 'Mummy,' she said, 'I was just praying to Jesus to make your bones better, when suddenly I saw a very bright light and I knew that everything was going to be all right.' It was on that very day that something remarkable happened to me. The rheumatoid arthritis which had crippled me began to retreat and my whole life was to take on a new direction. It is this healing and all that flows from it that I want to share, with the hope that my experiences can help and encourage other people.

My story takes place mainly in Lugwardine, a small village north east of Hereford, which sits on a hill above the river Lugg and is the home of one branch of the family of Thomas Traherne, the seventeenth-century mystical poet. Although Thomas himself did not live in the village, he commemorates it in verse:

> O yonder is the Moon
> Newly com after me to Town,
> That shin'd at Lugwardin but yesternight
> Where I enjoy'd the self-same Light.

I began life in Reading. I was delivered, feet first, by a Zen Buddhist on 12 March 1950, just in time for Sunday afternoon tea. The world I entered was that of an unusual and eccentric family, and I was the fourth and youngest child. My father was a remote figure during my early years, and I was very scared of him, not realising that he was also scared of me. In fact he was very fond of me, but was never able to show his affection by means of a kiss or an embrace; nevertheless I would frequently find him staring intently at me with an interested twinkle in his eye. During his last years, he would sit for long intervals watching my mother in the same way, undemonstrative but clearly appreciative. My father and mother were known respectively as Horse and Mare by family, friends and colleagues alike. The reason is lost in history, but the names were firmly established by the time I was born and I never knew them by any other. They frequently communicated with each other by a series of equine snorts and whinnies, intelligible only to themselves.

Horse dwelt in his study in the front of the house, surrounded on every wall by huge bookcases. Virtually every corner of the house was furnished with a bookcase, and there must have been nine or ten thousand volumes spilling over into passages, the kitchen and up two flights of stairs. His mantelpiece housed a collection of icons and other artefacts, which I do not believe were ever dusted in all the time that I knew that room. During my earliest years, Horse kept on that mantelpiece a jar of leeches, which squirmed and wriggled in accordance with the weather. Later he progressed to treefrogs, which lived in a glass case in one corner of the study, but these were once or twice found dead under bookcases, so that interest also passed.

When I was two years old, Horse contracted tuberculosis. He never fully recovered his health and for most of the years that I knew him, he was sick and in considerable pain. Ultimately he was forced to retire early. By profession he was a teacher of philosophy; he held the chair at Reading University, but most of his writing was theological. He began life in Sheffield as a Methodist, but became an Anglican during his student days in Oxford. He maintained his interest in the Methodists throughout his life and was also very deeply involved in relations with the Eastern Orthodox churches. As a family we belonged to the Anglican-Orthodox Fellowship of St Alban and St Sergius. Our summer holiday each year was to attend the annual conference, where Horse always lectured. For some years this was held by the sea at Broadstairs and was the high spot of my year. I loved the people, I loved the fellowship of the various denominations and nationalities, I loved the sense of structure and belonging that it gave to my life and I still love the many friends that it gave me. It seems very appropriate that the Fellowship also gave me a husband, having several years earlier provided my brother, Paul, with his wife Mary.

As Horse grew gradually weaker and less mobile, he spent less and less of his time at the University and began to wind down his responsibilities in preparation for his retirement. Even after retirement he would sit up late into the night reading, writing and listening to music and finally, having toured the house to lock the doors, he would go up to bed in the early hours of the morning.

Shortly after this, my mother would whirr into action. She inhabited the attic at the top of the house, completely surrounded by makeshift bookcases, cardboard boxes, papers and heaven knows what else. This chaos was paradise for the constant supply of kittens that our cat Persephone regularly produced. Many of them were born in cardboard boxes, all of them learned how to disrupt carefully sorted piles of papers, and much of Mare's writing was personally autographed by delicately placed paw-marks.

Mare was anything but conventional as a mother. Her cooking was abominable and she had no interest in sewing, but she was splendid on practical matters. When I was about seven years old, she built a boat, a little flat-ended dinghy called a Gremlin. We named it Hamid, after a fictional golden hamster, and spent many happy hours on canals, rivers and gravel pits.

Most of my early memories of Mare were of her writing and studying almost compulsively. She would study Hebrew in the early hours of the morning when most of us are not fit for studying anything. By day she taught English and R.K. at a

3

girls' grammar school in Reading; she had an extensive knowledge of English literature and a great love of language. As I write this, she is now in her early seventies and still studying and writing with the same persistence.

The rest of the family consisted of my two brothers, the cat, generations of kittens and several hamsters.

My elder brother, Wilfrid, was nine years older than I and already away at choir-school in Oxford by the time I was born. He did not feature very much in my earliest memories, but I grew to know him better when, before my own marriage, I lived with him and his wife Helen and their children in London.

Next came Paul, four years my senior, who also went off to choir-school before I was very old. He used to stay at school over Christmas to sing in the cathedral, and I remember helping Mare to make up a parcel of assorted presents and surprises to send to the choir boys each year.

After Paul came Catherine, but sadly she lived for only a few weeks. She was found dead in her cot at lunch-time on the one day that Horse had decided to change his routine and come home early to be with my mother. After Catherine's death, Mare climbed a ladder, by way of occupational therapy, and painted Greek inscriptions around the walls in the kitchen and in the front hall. In the kitchen, in red, she painted the last verse of 'the Day of Resurrection', 'Now let the heavens be joyful and earth her song begin. . .'. In the hall, in green, we had a text from the book of Joshua, 'I and my house will serve the Lord because he is holy.' It seemed quite normal to me to have Greek written around the walls, but it puzzled other people and always made a good talking point.

The church where we worshipped in Reading and where I was baptised, was High Church and this together with regular attendances at Orthodox liturgies caused me to grow up with a great love of the smell of incense. I used to watch the sunlight streaming down through the clerestory windows and feel myself being drawn up the shafts of light with the incense as it swirled and billowed towards the roof. I remember once being jolted back to reality to find Mare heaving with mirth. She had just heard the curate announce during his sermon that 'Not all the dogness in the world can extinguish the life of one small cat'. We later decided that he must have said 'Not all the darkness in the world can extinguish the light of one small candle', but we preferred the former version.

As a child I was very pious but I had a very private kind of spirituality and did not feel it was the done thing to talk about it or share it with anybody. I was often intensely aware of an overwhelming presence of good and then again of evil, but I never spoke about these experiences. I think I believed that no one would either understand or believe me. In spite of this piety I was very much afraid of God and believed that he really belonged only to the learned and the wise. Theological problems were tossed to and fro over the table at meal times, and at Fellowship conferences, scores of people would gather to argue, discuss, reargue and rediscuss this God. How could a child hope to understand this complicated being, whose true nature was so elusive even to the theologians? Jesus himself was barely presented to me, and it was not till I had my own children that I really came to know and understand him; and most important to love him and not be afraid of him.

At the age of nine I was sent away to school in North Wales. Most of the girls came from families involved in business, and I was singled out and bullied because I came from an academic background. I was desperately unhappy and my work and my self-confidence suffered severely. Four times during one summer term I was put in the school sanatorium just for my own protection. The system seemed to have no other way of resolving the problem. I now recognise that, at the age of twelve, I teetered on the edge of a complete nervous breakdown. Finally, when I was thirteen, I was transferred to a school nearer home, in Berkshire. I was tolerably happy there, but only partially regained my confidence.

It was during my last term at school, in the middle of a German dictation, that a sharp and violent pain shot through my abdomen. I was told I could leave the lesson and go to the sick-room. There was no reason to suspect that this heralded the beginning of many years of illness.

I climbed the stairs to the sickroom to find Matron, a fierce dragon of a woman who had the entire school under her thumb. She put me to bed with a pain-killer and came back again some hours later to ask how I was. I told her that I was still in pain, but she snapped at me and told me it was impossible. One did not argue with Matron, it was more than one's life was worth.

The following day I was examined by the school doctor, who diagnosed an ovary problem and prescribed iron pills. He always prescribed iron pills. They came in all shapes, sizes and colours, but they were all undeniably iron pills and they did nothing for the pain. I was unwell throughout the summer holidays, but assorted hospital tests and examinations revealed nothing.

When the autumn came, I began studying for my A-levels at Reading Technical College. On the first day, while sitting in a classroom with several others looking as lost and bewildered as myself, I was approached by an Indian girl, who asked me if she were in the right place. Her name was Baljeet and she had come from Kenya to study in England, where one sister was already a doctor and another was studying dentistry. We became close friends and after a while she moved out of her digs and came to live with me and my family. Wilfrid had already married and left home, so Baljeet was able to use his room. She immediately fitted into our eccentricities and we all loved her. Some years earlier Persephone had received the higher cat-call, and in current feline residence there was a neurotic and highly-strung Siamese cat named Morgan Le Fay. At first Baljeet had no interest in cats, but Morgan gradually won her over until, after some time, she admitted to liking them.

During my A-level year, I was still very uncertain what I wanted to do with my life. My German was good, but I did not feel that a degree in the language was what I wanted. I also thought that in such an academic family, it was time that someone did something practical; I therefore decided to study photography at the Berkshire College of Art.

Throughout the course I never really felt well. I was still having abdominal pain, and periodically one or other of my wrists would become weak and painful. This always passed over, but was very debilitating while it lasted. Baljeet was not strong either. She was born with a complicated heart condition, so together we were forced to take life quite gently.

During the summer of 1968, my first year at Art College, the Lambeth Conference was being held in London and the Fellowship conference was buzzing with visitors and overseas bishops. It was known that I was studying photography and I was asked if I would take photographs of the visiting bishops. I approached one bishop to ask his permission to take some photographs. He called over a young theology graduate to talk to him while I did so. This young man was tall and lean, with a mop of blond hair. His name was Stephen Parsons, and I instinctively felt I would see him again one day.

We met two years later at my nephew's baptism. Stephen and my brother Paul were spasmodically in touch, and Stephen had been asked to be a godfather. He had just been ordained deacon and was feeling very self-conscious about wearing his collar for the first time outside his parish. It was five years before we met again.

When I had finished the photography course, I spent a rather abortive year in Bradford, training to teach English as a second language. I had become very closely involved with the Asian immigrant community in Reading and spent a vast amount of my time photographing weddings, new babies,

8

families, cricket matches and circumcision ceremonies. This encouraged me to believe that I might enjoy teaching, but the year in Bradford convinced me and my tutors that this was not my calling.

I returned to photography and freelanced, working mainly for the Community Relations Commission, which sent me all over the country, photographing the activities and work being done among the immigrant communities in the big cities. For some time I had been studying Urdu, and with Baljeet's help and constant correction, I managed a passable fluency. After a year of freelancing, it was suggested that if I could get myself to India, the Commission would buy all the photographic work that I might bring home. Pictures of everyday life in India were constantly in use for educational purposes, and they needed as much as I could produce. This suggestion coincided with my twenty-first birthday, and I was given generous gifts of money to pay my fare. It also coincided with Baljeet's father's plan to visit India, so we arranged to stay with his relatives in Delhi and meet out there. I was very fortunate to have him as my guide and travelling companion, and my time in India is a memory that I treasure.

On returning to England, I obtained a job as a medical photographer at an orthopaedic hospital in London. The work was interesting but not very varied. There was the scoliosis clinic on Monday mornings and for the rest of the week I photographed femoral heads, patellae and literally hundreds of X-rays. There was also the occasional trip to the operating theatre and projectionist duties during lectures to doctors.

One incident stays in my mind very vividly. It was by no means the most tragic or the most gory of cases, but it has continued to haunt me and, in later years, I was able to identify with it closely. A woman, perhaps in her late forties, with very bad arthritis in her shoulders, had come into hospital to have one of the joints replaced. She was sent down to the photographic department, so that we could

9

record the fact that pre-operatively her movement was very limited. One of my colleagues took the case, and when she had undressed he asked her to raise her arm. After a few seconds, it became clear that she was in considerable pain and could not raise her arm any higher. The photographer became irritable and kept on insisting that she try harder; when at last she broke down and collapsed in tears into a chair, he stamped out of the room and slammed the door. I was left to try to comfort the woman and apologise for my colleague's behaviour.

Ten years later I was to experience the same pain and the same tears and I have often remembered that patient and that appalling incident.

After almost a year of working at this hospital, I began to have pains again in my abdomen and ultimately they became so severe that I was taken by my brother, Wilfrid, to the casualty department of a hospital in North West London. Within hours, I was operated on and the surgeon found several cysts on my right ovary and also signs of endometriosis. The mess was cleared up and I was assured that I would have no further trouble.

While convalescing I noticed that this hospital was advertising for a medical photographer, so I applied for the job and, within a month, had begun working there. I spent four very happy years in that department. The work was fascinating, I enjoyed the close contact that I had with the patients and I had marvellous colleagues.

As regards my health however, they were very difficult years but I was fortunate indeed to have a boss who exercised infinite patience over my frequent and prolonged absences. Some months after the operation I began to have severe pain once more. My GP was sympathetic but the two of us found it impossible to convince the consultant that anything was wrong with me.

The next crisis struck when I was spending the weekend with my parents, who had by this time moved to Pangbourne, just west of Reading. I was taken into hospital in

Reading, where the surgical registrar opened me up and found the ovary to have prolapsed. It was put back in place and once again I returned to work. Somehow I never seemed to be well and the pain continued relentlessly. Several times I pleaded to have the ovary removed, but I was always told that I was too young to lose an ovary. I argued that I was too young to be permanently unwell, as this problem had been festering since I was sixteen and I was now twenty three. Eventually, in early 1974, the pain became so intense that I was taken into hospital in Reading, where the consultant removed the ovary. Several years, six hospital stays and three major operations were over and at last the pain was gone. I believed at the time that I had done my stint of illness and that for the rest of my life I was going to be strong and healthy. I had no reason to suspect otherwise.

My boss allowed me an extended convalescence, so I remained in Pangbourne for a while and lazed on the banks of the river Pang at a spot where I had frequently paddled as a child and where my own children were later to splash and play Pooh-sticks on the bridge. Horse had retired three years earlier and we would sit together, indulging ourselves by watching all the lunch-time children's programmes and discussing the respective merits of Trumpton and Camberwick Green.

As I became stronger I was aware that I was experiencing a very deep but intangible peace. I had never before felt so totally relaxed and at one with everything and I revelled in it. It did not last and one dreadful day I found myself standing at the kerbside in tears because the thought of crossing the road overwhelmed me with terror. I ran home and flung myself on to the bed and wept for hours. I had never heard of post-operative depression and certainly had never been warned about it. My GP was very understanding and told me that this was common, particularly after the up-heaval of a gynaecological operation. He gave me some anti-depressant drugs and, feeling very groggy, I returned to work. The joy of having shed the physical pain was totally dissipated by this gloom which I carried around with me. By Christmas I had become very unstable and, on impulse, I threw in my job and went home to Pangbourne, where I sat and looked at the carpet for several weeks, completely devoid of any motivation. I had long since stopped taking any drugs because I disliked the effect they had on me and also because I wanted to fight the depression through my own resources.

It was some time before I felt confident enough to look for another job. Several medical photography posts were being advertised in London hospitals so I applied for four and was offered all of them. This boosted my confidence but it soon sank when I realised that I could not cope with a new situation and strange faces. So I returned to my former place of work and was welcomed with open arms by my boss, who knew and understood me better than I realised and had kept the post open for me. I could never have survived those years without his quiet support.

The next few months passed without incident and then the summer came bringing with it the return of Stephen into my life. We met briefly and formally at a dinner party at my brother's house and he enquired tentatively if I would be going to the Conference of the Fellowship of St Alban and St Sergius the following month. I had missed the conference through illness several years running and was feeling out of touch. I calculated that I could reach the place where the conference was taking place, as it was within one hour's drive from the hospital. So I borrowed Horse's rickety red van and set off one afternoon after work. The drive took me past fields and fields of golden grain, which were being harvested by cheerful red combines, and I thought the world was looking more beautiful than I had ever known it. Every evening for a week I drove past these fields and sat patiently behind trundling tractors for miles on end along the twisting roads.

By the end of the week we realised that everyone at the conference had been busy arranging our marriage. We kept quiet about the fact that we had too.

At this time Stephen was in Oxford, doing post-graduate research. He had already spent several years in a parish, but had decided to return to university for two years to write a thesis finishing off the studies that he had begun in Greece some years before. He was also working as a part-time curate in North Oxford.

I left my job, finally this time, and returned to Pangbourne to be within easy distance of Oxford. Stephen immediately found a great deal in common with Horse and Mare and Mare sealed her approval by handing him a small sick Communion set, which had belonged to her father and grandfather before. 'I think this belongs to you now', she said.

Shortly after I arrived in Pangbourne our next-door neighbour asked me if I would travel with him to the north of England to photograph a wall. I said yes, I should be delighted to photograph a wall, so we set out at six o'clock one morning. Some hours later I found myself standing at the perimeter wall of a top-security prison. This was the first of several visits to top security prisons around the country: my brief was to photograph security devices and buildings. On one occasion I was locked into a cell and had to photograph the door being blasted open, to demonstrate the procedure used when inmates barricade themselves inside their cells. On another occasion, I was hoisted to the top of a prison wall and had to climb along a little way inside the domed structure to take photographs. I confess to having no head for heights, and when I looked down, I was aware not only of the distance between myself and the ground, but also of the large white gleaming teeth of the fierce but very beautiful Alsatian dogs who escorted me everywhere on prison premises. I was as nervous of these dogs as I was of sitting at the top of a prison wall, and the wolf-whistles of the inmates on recreation on the other side of the wall did little to steady my nerves. It was an interesting experience but one that I would not be in a hurry to repeat.

The Home Office work carried me through until just before

Christmas, when I obtained a medical photography post in an Oxford hospital, a few hundred yards down the road from the hostel where Stephen was living. The hostel was an ecumenical centre founded by a member of the Fellowship of St Alban and St Sergius, and my brother Wilfrid had been one of the first students to live there. Now Stephen had a room on the other side of the house, which looked out over the Orthodox church.

Every morning I would leave Pangbourne early and drive to Oxford in time for a breakfast of steaming porridge, which Stephen would have ready for me. Very often I would spend the lunch hour with him and sometimes we would use the hour to go to auctions and look for cheap but serviceable furniture.

Originally we planned to marry in the autumn, when Stephen had finished his thesis and was back in a parish, but the offer of a college flat came up and was too good to ignore. I was also very much aware how desperately ill Horse was, and I had a feeling deep down that if we waited till autumn he would no longer be alive. So with the security of a flat to live in we married in April. On the morning of the wedding, Horse was clearly very weak. We had already arranged that Wilfrid should give me away and Horse bravely agreed to attend the reception and give his speech. It was a literary work of art and in the many letters that my mother later received, the sentiment was repeated over and over again, 'How wonderful to hear the Horse lecture again.' This was the last time that he ever appeared in public and two months later he died. I truly believe that he had stayed alive to see us married and had then meekly given in to sickness and finally death.

In the autumn of 1976 we left Oxford and moved down to Ramsgate, where Stephen was to be curate of a parish church and priest-in-charge of two daughter churches. We were given a house conveniently near the station, and I had a wonderful neighbour on one side, who loved a bit of friendly gossip over the wall whilst hanging out the washing.

By this time I was already pregnant and feeling thoroughly nauseous. I would sit outside and inhale vast quantities of sea air and convince myself that this was doing me good. I used to lie in bed at night and listen to the fog-horns from the lightships out on the Goodwin Sands and remember how I had loved those same foghorns as a child when I had stayed at Broadstairs, a little further round the coast. My pregnancy advanced without major incident and in the spring Anna was born, in a room which looked out over a field of best Thanet cabbages.

She was a happy and easy little baby and she smiled a great deal at everybody and at life in general. In spite of this I was becoming increasingly aware that the depression I thought had gone for ever was slowly creeping in on me; I realised that I must have the post-natal depression which I had frequently read about. I was not eager to take anti-depressant drugs, but I was frightened of not being able to take care of a small baby if I sank too low. A psychiatrist came to see me and suggested that I have a brief spell in hospital, in order to have ECT treatment. I recoiled in horror and flatly refused. As with the post-operative depression three years earlier, I realised that I should have to fight this on my own, with Stephen's help of course, but the depression was changing course in a rather alarming fashion.

Ever since childhood I had suffered from psychic disturbances and from about the age of seven onwards I would periodically wake in the night screaming in the belief that I was being dragged out of bed by some force. So powerful was this force that I was always amazed to find that I was still in bed and not on the floor. These incidents had died down during my early twenties but it was clear that they were now trying to work their way to the surface again. Now I was experiencing the same terror and the same sensation of being dragged from my bed and Stephen, woken by my screams, would have to pray with me to calm me down before I could fall asleep again. These disturbances became more frequent and I became increasingly tired and depressed.

Anna continued to smile and her happy disposition assured me that she was not being affected by my problems, but I was worried about the effect that all this could have on the three of us. Stephen desperately wanted to help me, but I was becoming so mixed up and confused that I found it impossible to discuss anything with the one person closest to me. I had read a fair amount on depression and had learned of a priest in another part of the country who had been able to help a number of people suffering from problems similar to my own. I therefore made an appointment to go and see him and arrived at his doorstep one golden autumn day.

I was ushered into his study, where we talked for a while and I was puzzled by the fact that he appeared to be suffering intermittently from a sort of petit-mal. After an hour or so of discussion, he took me into the church and I knelt down at the altar rail. I began to feel uncomfortable without understanding why, and from the moment he placed his hands on my head, there began one of the most terrifying experiences that I have ever had. The large hanging lights on the ceiling rattled on their chains and the west door creaked open and slammed shut with a force that shook my whole body. The priest then led me down the church and showed me the west door and the yale lock that secured it. 'That noise was the evil leaving,' he told me, but I was not convinced and felt that, in some extraordinary way, he himself was the source of these theatrical but sinister happenings. He told me that my eyes shone with a new peace, but I was almost stiff with terror and could hardly wait to escape. After a parting handshake I ran all the way down the road and did not stop until I reached the station.

I arrived home late and exhausted and fell straight into bed, hoping to forget the events of the day in a deep sleep. This was not to be. After a short and shallow sleep I woke screaming because I had felt someone touching me on the shoulder and tugging at my hair. As soon as Stephen was awake the presence disappeared; Stephen put his arm round me and prayed with me and again I fell asleep. Perhaps an hour later I woke to the sound of a ghostly and devilish laughter, which seemed to fill my head and the whole room. I shook Stephen awake and immediately the laughter subsided. The night continued like this and Stephen and I realised that whatever else had happened in that church, the lid had certainly been taken off something very sinister.

The next evening Stephen had to go out to a meeting and I was alone in the kitchen preparing some baby-food for the following day. Suddenly I noticed that the scissors hanging on a hook above me were swinging round in ever increasing circles and then, one by one, all the kitchen utensils hanging along the same row began to rock and swing, gently at first and then gradually more violently. I fled upstairs and into Anna's bedroom and huddled on a stool next to her cot until Stephen came home. That night and for several successive nights I would wake screaming in the belief that something was pulling me from the bed and each time I could never understand why I was still in the bed when I awoke.

In my general terror and confusion I remembered a book that I had read, by a clergyman in London, and suddenly one afternoon I felt myself moved to go and see him. I left Stephen with the baby, ran the hundred yards up the road to the station and climbed onto the London train. It was already early evening when I arrived in London and I walked around for some time trying to find the vicarage, which had apparently been moved to another road. Eventually I was directed to the right house and I knocked at the door. The vicar's wife opened the door, looked at me, and without asking any questions took me in and sat me in front of a fire. Her husband appeared silently from nowhere and the two of them prepared some hot soup and sat quietly with me while I drank it and warmed myself. When his wife had left with the dishes, the clergyman spoke to me. 'You're frightened, aren't you?' I poured out the whole tale of the ghastly goings on over the previous few days. We talked for a while and he helped me to unravel and face up to all the turmoil and unhappiness that had built up inside me over the years and had contributed towards the deep depressions I had experienced past and present.

He stood up and indicated that we should go into the church together so I followed him silently, thinking all the while of my experience in another church only a few days before. Again I went and knelt down and put my hands on the altar rail in front of me; and immediately I felt hands on my head and I heard prayers being spoken over me. But this was very different. Suddenly I became aware of a second pair of hands; someone had placed their hands over mine on the altar rail. These hands were warm and comforting and I opened my eyes in amazement but there was no one there. I closed my eyes again and tried to recreate the feeling, it had been so wonderful, but this time I felt only a secure and loving presence around me. I knew from that moment that God was with me whatever I was to go through. That brief touch on my hands was momentary but it had spoken volumes.

When I returned home I knew that the lid had been replaced on the sinister events of the past few days but I was still depressed and I still periodically woke screaming in the night. I visited that clergyman on many occasions and I believe that he was a major source of help to me during my depression.

By the beginning of the next year, 1978, I noticed some pain and swelling in the index and middle fingers of my right hand. As I am left-handed, this did not cause too much of a problem at first, but the pain increased and after a while I found that trying to fasten a nappy pin was almost impossible. My GP took a blood sample and when the result came back he informed me, almost casually, that I had rheumatoid arthritis. He did not appear to be at all alarmed or surprised, so at first I took my cue from him and tried not to be too concerned about it. I knew virtually nothing about the disease, but I kept remembering the appalling and painful deformities that I had photographed in the past. One of the greatest blows was that I was now finding it very difficult to play the recorder. I had grown up in a very musical family, but I had stopped playing the piano when my lack of confidence told me that competing against two brothers who played brilliantly was pointless. Stephen helped me to rebuild my confidence in many ways, but in particular he encouraged me to take up the recorder again, so I played and played and managed to reach quite a reasonable standard and most of all to enjoy it enormously.

When the summer came, we attended the Fellowship conference and several of us made up a small medieval music group. We met every morning after breakfast and at the end of the week played a few pieces at the closing annual concert. When we played together in the mornings, my fingers were very stiff and painful and I was increasingly frightened that I would have to give up playing the recorder. I told no one of the arthritis and kept these fears to myself.

For some weeks I had been visiting a man in the parish who claimed to have a natural gift of healing. He would hold my fingers in his hand and mutter to himself in Latin, but after a while he lost interest in my fingers and I found my visits to him consisted of his talking endlessly about himself. Then he took to ringing me up every evening, always at the time I was putting Anna to bed, and always expecting me to drop everything and listen to him for as long as he chose to talk. I realised that he was very lonely, but I was not personally in a position to help, others having tried and failed, and so I severed the contact.

As the year drew on and autumn approached, we discovered with great happiness that I was pregnant again. Anna gave us such pleasure, and we looked forward to having another baby. When I emerged from the initial sickness, I noticed that the pain and swelling in my fingers was gradually subsiding and by the time I was well into the pregnancy they had returned to normal. I noticed, and Stephen did also, that I did not seem so depressed. The nightmares were becoming fewer and further apart, and I was starting to talk about the future with a greater confidence.

4

During the spring Stephen received a letter asking him if he would be interested in looking at a parish near Hereford. For some months he had been anticipating a move, and this approach came through the recommendation of a friend of his in the Hereford diocese. The parish was called Lugwardine with Bartestree, and although we had no idea how to pronounce the first half, it sounded promising. It happened that the following day we went to stay at Pangbourne, and Stephen and Mare suddenly decided that they would set out early the next morning and go and look at the place. I was seven months pregnant and did not feel like travelling so I stayed at home with Anna. When they had driven for quite some time and felt that they would soon drop off the edge of England, they reached the Malverns and the signposts began to mention Hereford. On their arrival in Lugwardine, the weather was very overcast but they got out of the car briefly and looked at the church and peered over the vicarage wall. The bank in the garden was covered in primroses, the flowers I had chosen for my wedding bouquet, and there was the odd plant or two in the churchyard. Stephen returned home and replied to the letter saying that he would be delighted to come and look at the parish. Some six weeks later everything was settled; we would be moving to Lugwardine in September, when the new baby would be three months old.

During the week before the expected date of delivery, my friend Margaret came and stayed with us and took over the household. Anna had arrived a week early and we suspected that this one might do the same, so Margaret was there just in case, but nothing happened, except that Anna developed

21

quite severe chickenpox. A few hours after Margaret's departure for a wedding in Cambridge, I noticed the first signs of labour but the hospital was not willing to admit me because of Anna's illness. Their compromise was to put me in isolation and send the occasional masked nurse to peer round the door at me. It was very peaceful being in isolation and in the early hours of the next morning, with only Stephen and the midwife present, Clare squawked her way into our lives. There were no cabbages in the fields at this time of year, but the seagulls were whirling and screaming to herald her arrival.

We were very happy to have a second girl; in fact I had always secretly hoped for two girls. In the past, when I had worked among Asian immigrants, I had been told many a time by Moslems that 'Allah will give you many sons', but Allah had obviously understood my preference and decided otherwise. Clare was eccentric from the start. She sported a magnificent punk hair-style, which stuck up at right angles from her head, and wore a puzzled expression underneath it. Anna was very proud of her and enjoyed being useful.

One night, when Clare was six weeks old, I leaned over her cot to lift her out. I then suddenly became aware of a stabbing pain in my shoulder, which subsided into a dull ache. During my pregnancy I had completely forgotten about the rheumatoid arthritis. I still did not know anything about the behaviour of the disease and I was not even sure that the pain in my shoulders was connected, but it was sufficient to frighten me. As the days progressed, the pain increased and began to spread through my body. First my wrists, then my hands and feet were affected. The pain was not stable in any one place for long but darted about through my limbs and across my shoulders. I would wake very stiff in the mornings and take a while to unfold. I managed to cope during the day, but then experienced stabbing pains again by evening.

I started packing for the move early so that I could do a little at a time. Lifting was becoming more and more difficult because of the pain in my shoulders, and on occasions I had to ask Stephen to lift Clare out of her cot. I worried that I might not be able to do much to help during the move, so I tried to do as much sorting out and packing as possible to make things easy for Stephen.

An additional worry at this time was that Clare was very colicky and cried a great deal in the evenings. I bought a sling so that I could carry her on my front and for a while this helped and comforted her but my shoulders could not take the weight, even of a small baby, and the pain forced me to abandon the idea.

The day of the move arrived and when I had shaken off the initial stiffness I realised that I was in fact managing quite well, though getting tired easily. When everything was finally bolted up inside the removal van, we set off independently for Pangbourne where we spent the night before starting early the next morning for Lugwardine.

It was a drizzly day when we drove to our new home. I had worried that we would not have enough goods and chattels to fill such a big house, but we soon filled up every available corner with bookcases and still more bookcases. As vicarages go it was not really so big, but compared with our previous house it seemed simply colossal, and it took me quite some time to get used to travelling vast distances to answer the telephone or the door bell.

We had three weeks to settle in before Stephen's induction as Vicar; which we used for two purposes. As the interior was badly in need of redecoration and as I enjoy painting, I opted to stay at home and cover as many walls as possible, with Clare watching from her little chair and blowing the occasional bubble. Stephen and Anna went out to explore the countryside in all directions, and Anna particularly enjoyed their trips into Wales to look for red dragons in the mountains. I found that I could manage reasonably well with the painting, but by the evening my shoulders were always very painful. Mercifully my knees were not yet involved and I was still able to kneel and do things at floor level. One evening I was kneeling on the bathroom floor, putting down some lino, when sudden and violent pains shot through my legs. I tried to stand up and found my legs giving way under me. This began to happen regularly in the evenings, and I was worried that I would have the same problem on the night of Stephen's induction.

By this time I had registered with a doctor in Hereford. One of our church wardens was a GP, two years short of retirement, and I asked his advice on doctors, telling him that I was anxious to get the children registered, particularly as Clare was now due for several injections. I said nothing about my physical condition or my very great fears. He put me in touch with a friend of his, a GP in town, and I registered the whole family with him. When the children were up-to-date with their immunisations, I spoke to him about my own problem. He was an extremely kind man and I liked him immediately. He told me that he was not entirely sure that my symptoms were behaving like those of rheumatoid arthritis, but he took a blood sample and asked me to come back and see him in a week's time.

The day before the return visit was the day of the Induction. Both our mothers came to stay, and an assortment of friends, relations and former parishioners turned up to share the occasion with us. To my relief, my legs behaved quite well and I was able to hide from everybody the fact that anything was wrong. On the following morning a number of people gathered at the house before their departures, but I had somehow to escape and get to my doctor's appointment. Of course, everyone was concerned to know what was wrong with me so I told them that this was a rather belated post-natal check-up.

When I entered the GP's surgery, he looked up gravely and waved me to a chair. He sorted through my notes and extracted the offending piece of paper, saying, 'I really am sorry, Frances, but this result confirms that you have rheumatoid arthritis'. I have no clear memory of my re-action; I think I was very stunned and I also believe that I still did not fully understand the implications. The doctor reached for his notepad and as he wrote he said, 'I'm sending you to a specialist; she's very good.' He told me that I would be sent notice of a hospital appointment and advised me to take aspirin for the pain and early morning stiffness. When I returned home, one or two visitors were still about, but I slipped past them and went upstairs to my room where I sat on the bed in numbed disbelief. I had been through so much illness already; I had battled my way through gynaecological problems, depression and psychic disturbances, and I was still only in my twenties. Why did I have to go through yet another illness and yet more pain? How on earth was I going to cope with two small children and a large vicarage?

Stephen was caught up with various people on the point of leaving and making their farewells, so my mother came upstairs to find me and sat down on the bed next to me. I told her the details of the last few weeks and of my visit to the doctor and of why I had not told her about it earlier. I felt, unfairly, that my family must have become as weary of all my illnesses as I had, and in a sense I was embarrassed to present them with yet another one. I asked Mare to keep my arthritis a secret until such time as it became obvious, and she gave me her word.

The nature of the disease was now beginning to alter. The fleeting pains had stopped chasing up and down my limbs and the pain became mainly concentrated in the joints. At this stage the only joints exempt from pain and swelling were my elbows and knees; even my jaw was involved and I found mealtimes perfectly miserable. My fingers were becoming swollen and they stiffened up in only a few minutes if I was not using them. I found it increasingly difficult to manage buttons and fastenings, and trying to dress Clare and fasten nappies became at times so difficult that I just had to hand her over to Stephen. By far the most painful joints were those of my shoulders; I had never before realised how extensively the shoulders are involved in our minute-by-minute use of our whole bodies. Every movement, every action, walking, sitting or lying caused my shoulders to scream out their protest, and I became thoroughly exhausted with the pain. I was no longer able to carry Anna and even Clare I could only lift for a few seconds at a time.

This was the greatest pain of all; I had two beautiful little daughters, whom I could no longer carry. When my instincts told me to lift them and cuddle them, my body protested violently. Anna began to sense this and before long she was waking in the night and calling for Daddy. She was falling down and running to Daddy. She was taking all her problems to Daddy. At first this hurt me very deeply, although I knew that I could not get out of bed at night or lift her up when she fell over. But gradually I began to realise how lucky she was to have a Daddy who was so willing and available, and how lucky I was to have a husband who was so loving and supportive; the hurt faded and turned into acceptance and gratitude. Anna was now a few months short of three years old and being a very gregarious little person, was in need of more company. We found a playgroup in Hereford which took children from the village and she was accepted at once. From her first visit she settled in well and for three mornings a week she played, sang and made ingenious little artefacts out of cardboard clutter.

Clare, now six months old, had come through her earlier colicky stage but was very clinging and unwilling to leave me even for a moment. Perhaps she sensed my problems and felt insecure because of them. Basically she was a very happy little baby, but only on condition that she was with me all the time.

At the beginning of the new year 1980, I at last received notification of my first hospital appointment and I set off for the hospital, wondering what I would learn both about the disease and about treatment. The specialist seemed keen to start me on a course of gold injections. She obviously sensed my initial reluctance and told me to think about it for a fortnight, meanwhile trying an anti-inflammatory drug. During this fortnight I did a bit of research and discovered both people who had been helped and also those who had not been helped by gold treatment. The anti-inflammatory drug was having no effect and the pain, particularly in my shoulders, was increasing, so, urged on by my GP, I returned to the hospital and agreed to start the treatment. For some weeks I did not notice any particular change, but by the time we were well into the spring, I realised that after a measure of stiffness in the morning I was virtually unaware of the arthritis during the daytime.

During May we took advantage of my new-found mobility and took the children many times into the Welsh mountains. Our most memorable day was the occasion when Anna, aged three and a half and completely unassisted, climbed to the top of the Skirrid, 2500 feet. Stephen carried Clare on his back and Anna bounced on yards ahead of the rest of us. It was quite cold and very windy, but I felt a wonderful sense of achievement because I had reached the top. Alas, this happy state was short-lived, and as the summer approached, the stiffness and disability crept back slowly but emphatically. This time my fingers and wrists were badly affected; my wrists became so weak and painful that even the most simple tasks proved difficult and sometimes impossible.

The specialist suggested that I be fitted for some wrist splints. I visualised some ghastly contraptions rather like leg-irons attached to my arms, but in fact they were neat and attractively made in a soft leather, with concealed iron bars to strengthen the wrists. They were extremely comfortable to wear and an excellent support. If on occasions my wrists were knocked even slightly the pain would jar my whole arm with an unbelievable intensity, but inside the splints they were held secure and I felt much safer. In fact, people frequently admired the handsome leather splints and after a while I was not so bothered at having to wear them.

We had by this time been in the parish for a year and the telephone was ringing more and more frequently, particularly at the times when I was bathing the children, or having the rests for which I was feeling an increasing need; we therefore had a telephone installed in the bedroom. This revolutionised my life. My movements were slowing down, and a trip downstairs to answer the phone was often more than I could cope with. I also discovered that to answer the front door, I needed only to lean out of the bathroom window. This surprised the parishioners at first, but then they grew accustomed to ringing the door bell and then stepping back to look up at the bathroom window. My bedtime always followed closely upon the children's, as by early evening the constant arthritic pain and the liveliness of two small children had completely exhausted me. It was an enormous relief to be able to fall into bed knowing that neither the telephone nor the door bell need fetch me downstairs again.

With the end of June came an event I had been dreading for weeks. I had been asked to open the fête in a neighbouring village and had agreed because I felt too shy to refuse. There were one or two things I had vowed I would never do when I became a vicar's wife: wearing a hat was one of them and opening a fête was another. In the event I really quite enjoyed it. I had to judge a dog-show and a beauty-contest and the whole family were treated to a strawberry tea on the strength of it.

On the same day a GP and his family moved into the house through the field behind our own, and having children of comparable age, we quickly became friends. During conversation I learned that John was doing a certain amount of photography at the Eye Hospital and he indicated that there might be some part time work if I were interested. I toyed with the idea for a while, but my fingers were becoming increasingly stiff and painful and I realised that the handling of photographic equipment was really out of the question.

As my hands became less and less functional, I was determined to keep using them creatively. I remembered a wonderful friend of ours who at the age of seventy had gained a City and Guilds Diploma in embroidery. At the time I had been rather envious of her skill, as I was also very fond of any kind of needlework and had half promised myself that one day I would follow the same course. Now would seem to be the ideal time, and after some extensive research I tracked down a tutor who lived in an enormous house which nestled under Wenlock Edge in Shropshire, and was given over to the teaching of every kind of craft imaginable. The journey was a good hour in each direction but the tutor was talented in so many fields that I was determined to travel the distance in order to learn from her. For a while I managed to get to Shropshire fairly frequently, and Stephen was so keen I should continue that he changed his day off to enable me to be there on the day when the classes were held. I loved those days. I began to combine my passion for wild flowers with my interest in embroidery, and I had great plans for the things I was going to design and make for the City and Guilds exam and afterwards. The needlework hurt my fingers and my wrists, but I was not going to give in; I was going to keep my fingers active, however misshapen and swollen they were becoming.

I continued to visit the hospital regularly and to have the gold injections accompanied by a fast turn-over of anti-inflammatory drugs. By now I was relying almost exclusively on aspirin for pain relief, and my first action every morning was to down a mixture of soluble aspirin. It tasted horrid and brought me out in a sweat but it did help me to unstiffen and start moving. The mornings were becoming more and more difficult, and I was no longer able to get up and dress the children. In the evenings I would put out their clothes for the next day and Stephen would dress them and make their breakfast. Sometimes he would have to dress me as well. I could not lift my shoulders without considerable pain, and I found buttons impossible. Stephen would frequently have to ease me into my clothes in the morning and ease me out again at bedtime. Of course, the people in the parish now knew about my arthritis, as it had become obvious from the way I moved. For a long time I had told no one but Jess, the churchwarden's wife, and Sheila, my neigh-

29

bour. Both of them were wives of doctors and both of them were a constant support to me mainly because they never fussed, but were always there when I needed help.

I found I was learning a great deal through my own illness about other people and their attitudes both to illness and to those who have it. Everybody wanted to be kind, but so often their attempts came out as blatant tactlessness. Day after day I was informed, 'You're much too young to have this disease', and day after day I was told, 'It'll burn out one day'. This constant reminder that I was too young to be so ill was hurtful and very far from helpful, and never had I heard officially from a doctor that the disease would 'burn out' or indeed had ever heard of anyone to whom this had happened. I developed a polite exterior smile in answer to these perennial statements, but inside I wept.

Stephen collected a lot of literature on rheumatoid arthritis and read far more than I did. He would frequently come home from visiting in the parish with the news that Mrs So-and-So's great aunt was helped by such and such a remedy. Many of the suggestions seemed rather improbable, but Stephen's determination to make me better was relentless and without him I could easily have put my head down and given up. I worked my way through several folk-remedies, but with no success. We kept hearing about diets that had helped people, so Stephen went out and bought a number of recipe books and I embarked on my first diet. It entailed eating quite a lot of fish and as I have an intense dislike for any kind of fish, I did not enjoy the regime very much. I kept to it for quite a long time and it did make me feel more alert, but it had no effect on the arthritis. In all, I tried some four or five recommended diets but the indication was that help for me did not lie in this direction. There was, however, no doubt in my mind that diet had helped several individuals I knew, but I had to seek elsewhere for a solution.

5

At about this time, early in 1981, I learned that healing services were held regularly in our district. For some reason, I have no memory why, I set off for a service feeling cross and with absolutely no expectations. Once in church I continued to feel cross, and the rather tinkly sentimental music only irritated me further. Towards the end of the service, we all filed up to the altar rail for the laying-on-of-hands and I found myself kneeling at the feet of a visiting retired priest. As he placed his hands on my head I suddenly became aware of a very powerful force, which appeared to be drawing away from me and up through his hands. I felt intensely dizzy and had to check my balance so that I did not keel over. As I returned to my seat, I realised that my anger, whatever it had been, had vanished and I went home feeling mildly ashamed.

The next day was my birthday and I got up and dressed slowly and painfully as always, but something was different. It was my normal custom to reach for my splints immediately on waking as my wrists were too weak and painful to manage without them but this morning I had not done so. My wrists seemed stronger and it appeared that I could do the lighter tasks without them.

I began to attend the healing services regularly, but became increasingly disenchanted for a number of reasons. I sensed a cosiness which was not compatible with challenge and apart from a dedicated few who attended regularly to pray for the sick, I sensed a lack of expectation. The clergy worked according to a rota and I know that a number of them were committed and approached the services prayerfully, but I also believe that a number did not. I place my head on the block when I say that I am aware of a clerical arrogance which states, 'I am an ordained priest of God therefore I have the authority to lay on hands and heal', and I speak for the multitudes of sick people on the receiving end, whose opinions are rarely asked for. We do have the sensitivity to know who is approaching our healing with prayer and with preparation and by the same token, we also have the sensitivity to detect otherwise.

On one occasion Stephen tried to make an appointment to see one of the clergy who periodically attended the healing services. He thumbed through his diary and said, 'No you can't see me on that date, there's a healing service – oh, never mind, I'll send one of the curates.' Possibly, indeed probably, the curate was a more appropriate person to administer the laying-on-of-hands, but this approach was casual in the extreme and for me was the final straw.

Throughout the spring I battled with diets and was clearly losing. In spite of an endless assortment of drugs and an increasingly higher dose of gold, the activity of the disease was rising rapidly and the pain was exhausting me. My knees, which had held out for so long, were now becoming swollen and painful and occasionally caved in underneath me with no warning. Up till this time I had maintained the ability to walk reasonably well, but once my knees were affected, my mobility slowed down considerably. Eventually I was so unsteady on my legs that I could not walk safely without a stick. Mercifully I was still able to drive, although with great difficulty, and during the early summer I drove several times to a convent in Malvern, where I would spend time talking with one of the sisters there. A contact of Stephen's had pointed me in her direction, and certainly I found my visits valuable. We talked a lot and we laughed a lot and she helped me to untangle some of my spiritual and emotional muddle. After a while, however, I found the journey too long and too painful and I had to stop seeing her.

The summer was terrible. I barely walked and I rarely drove. I was spending days at a time immobilised by pain. My hands became so distorted that I had to take off my wedding ring, but I wore it on a chain around my neck because I wanted to keep it always about my person. It seemed ironic that in the Year of the Disabled I was myself becoming well and truly disabled.

For far too long I had tried to cope with the housework on my own and had refused to give up, even though I could not carry the vacuum cleaner up or downstairs. Every effort to do any cleaning reduced me to tears and confined me to bed to recover. Eventually I had to accept that I just could not manage and at last help arrived in two forms. First, the social services sent me a Home Help. She was a cheerful and extremely strong Welsh woman who blew through the house like a hurricane and left no corner untouched. Secondly a quiet, rather shy woman from our congregation offered to come in on Friday mornings. She asked if she could do this as her stewardship for the church and refused to let us pay her anything. She was as thorough as the Home Help, and between them they made the house look as it had never done when I was in charge. Anna and Clare adored both of them and when one or other was in the house Stephen would use the opportunity to go out and do some visiting in the parish, knowing that the children and I would be all right for a while.

Sheila from next door came over frequently to collect the children while I rested, and I knew how lucky I was to have such a friend and neighbour, but I also worried because I could do so little for the children myself, and I felt I was a useless specimen of a mother. The children never complained. So many of their requests were greeted with the answer, 'I'm sorry I can't do that, you'll have to wait for Daddy to come home'. Perhaps they developed great patience, but it hurt me. I wanted to do so much for them and could do so little. The one thing I could give them was time and they would sit one on each side of me on the bed for hours while I read to them. Sometimes they were content just to be in the room with me and would carry their toys into the bedroom and play round me on the floor.

For some time a clergyman in the diocese had taken an interest in my welfare and visited me regularly to see how I was getting on. He spoke to me at length one day and told me that he would like to conduct a service of anointing for me. He suggested that I invite a few close friends and one or two clergy, and write to people I knew who would pray for me on that day. We fixed a date for the following week, 16 July, Stephen's birthday, and I gathered a group of people to be with me. I already knew that many people all over the country, mainly St Alban and St Sergius Fellowship contacts, regularly prayed for me, and I felt very humbled that so many people were so concerned for me. Rightly or wrongly, I always felt too shy to ask for my own healing and so it was a great support to me to know that I had the prayers of others.

The day, 16 July, arrived and I was feeling rough. I had been briefed beforehand to relax and let everyone else pray on my behalf and I remember going over to the church feeling vaguely detached but at the same time expectant. A group of about twelve people were assembled in the choir stalls and I limped up the aisle to join them. The priest officiating appeared from the vestry robed in splendid red and white vestments, and I remember thinking that if all this was being done just for me, surely God would respond in his own way. It was several weeks since I had been able to kneel but on this occasion I was determined to try. I did kneel, slowly and very painfully, and a number of the people present came and placed their hands on me while I was anointed with oil. I had imagined that I would re-experience the presence I had felt four years earlier in that church in London and I found myself yearning for the same reassuring touch on my hands but I felt nothing. The service ended with a celebration of Holy Communion after which we all adjourned to the vicarage for some coffee. I collected Anna and Clare from a friend who had been looking after them and then collapsed into a chair. I was exhausted.

34

Next day, 17 July, I realised that there was a very definite change in my condition. I was considerably worse. The pain in my legs was so intense that I could barely stand and my knees had swollen out of all recognition. A young doctor came out to visit me and prescribed a powerful anti-inflammatory drug which had an effect of some kind but not enough to allow me any mobility.

We began to think again about what should be our next move in our battle against my arthritis. For some time an acquaintance had been urging me to try acupuncture, as she had obtained much relief from her migraine through this treatment. Stephen thumbed through the Yellow Pages and found the telephone number of a man practising in a town about twenty-five miles distant. He telephoned and I was offered a cancelled appointment on the very next day.

The door was opened to me by a tall, serious looking gentleman who ushered me in with barely a word or a gesture. He waved me to a chair and then sat down with pen and notebook and began to ask a lot of questions. I found his questions entirely relevant to my particular situation and though his approach fresh and interesting. I felt he talked sensibly about arthritis and I heard none of the well-worn clichés I had grown to expect from people. He told me that on this occasion he was not going to treat the arthritis as such, but that he was going to treat me as a person. He could see that the pain was wearing me out both physically and emotionally and he explained that he wanted to channel my energy so that I would feel generally stronger. He plunged one needle into my tummy, one into the base of my big toe and one into my hand, leaving them there for about twenty minutes. When he removed the one from my left hand I suddenly realised that the fingers which I had been unable to bend for a long time were now malleable enough for me to form them slowly, if painfully, into a fist. The acupuncturist registered no surprise at all; he took such occurrences for granted, but I was very excited.

That evening, some time past my usual bedtime, I found

myself still pottering around doing various small jobs, and I realised that I did actually have a great deal more strength than I had had for a long time. This boost in stamina lasted for some months and was to help carry me through the very difficult period which lay ahead.

My GP, who was by now becoming increasingly concerned about my condition, supported my decision to have acupuncture treatment. He also gave in to my plea that I discontinue the gold injections, as I was experiencing unpleasant side-effects and my condition was obviously worsening despite the treatment. The rheumatology specialist was herself very ill at this time and had been away from work for some months so the GP decided to arrange a consultation for me with a specialist in London. I had to wait a few weeks as the man concerned was away on holiday.

During this time Baljeet came to stay, bringing her husband, a surgeon, and their baby daughter. Baljeet was not strong at all and she told me that during the next year she was hoping to have major heart surgery. So often our lives had run parallel; we decided that the following year was the year in which we would both get better, or at least begin to.

I was spending more and more time in bed, exhausted by the pain and immobilised by the swelling and deformities in my joints, and I was obviously able to do very little for the children. Anna was now four and a half and very bright and active. She was due to start school the following January as a rising five, but it was suggested to us by several people that we should try to get her into school in the approaching September. We wrote to the education authority and explained our position and our belief that Anna was quite ready to cope with school should she be allowed to start. The Chief Education Officer in Worcester contacted our GP, who supported us wholeheartedly, and a week or two later we received a courteous letter saying yes, Anna could certainly begin school in September, and the authorities hoped that this arrangement would help to lessen our problems. Anna was delighted, especially as her particular friend from playgroup was to start school at the same time. The village school was very conveniently at the bottom of our garden. A gate from the playground opened into the garden, or we could approach the school through the churchyard. This was ideal, as it allowed Stephen to be free from the responsibility of having to be home in order to collect Anna from school and although I was very lame, I could manage to get myself as far as the school gates. Anna settled in immediately; she loved her teacher and the work and we felt we had done the right thing for her.

In the second week of term I at last received notification of a consultation in London, and Stephen organised his time-table so that he could look after the children for about twenty four hours or so while I was away.

I travelled by train as far as Reading, where Mare met and joined me and together we continued the journey to London. When we arrived at Paddington, we found a very long queue of people waiting for taxis. I knew that I would find it far more difficult to stand and wait than I would to keep moving; I also knew that the walk from the tube station to the hospital at the other end was not very far, so Mare helped me down the steps to the tube and a train came in almost immediately.

I flopped down on to a seat, marvelling that I had managed to get this far, at the same time wishing that the ordeal were over and that I were safely back at home. I wanted to cry from the pain I was in and I was frightened of the crowds and of being pushed and jostled. As I looked up and began to focus on the people around me, I noticed at the far end of the carriage a shabbily dressed and extremely hairy man who was slowly working his way towards where Mare and I were sitting. He swayed slightly with the movement of the train and came to a halt immediately in front of me. Slowly he bent down and very gently took my face in his hands. 'Everything is going to be all right my love,' he whispered, 'everything is going to be all right.' His eyes twinkled through the mass of overgrowth on his face and with one

37

touch to my cheek he swayed back down the carriage. This man was not drunk, he neither spoke nor smelled as though he had been drinking; neither was his touch in any way lecherous and with my splints, my stick and my obviously haggard and pale appearance I was hardly attractive. The train rattled out of the tunnel and into a station and the man got up from his seat and moved towards the doors. Before leaving he hesitated and then came over to me again. As before he leaned forward, cupped his hands around my face and said, 'Don't worry my love, everything's going to be all right.' He left just before the automatic doors closed on him and ambled off down the platform and out of sight. The people sitting around me smiled indulgent and embarrassed smiles and through the buzz of conversation I could detect the words 'simple', 'potty' and 'raving-mad'. But was he? I still wonder.

The next stop was ours and we made our way slowly to the hospital. Only a few years earlier I had darted confidently across these roads and in and out of the traffic, but now the whole scene terrified me and I felt as so many elderly people must feel when surrounded by vast crowds and surging traffic.

When we reached the hospital I sent Mare off to find a bookshop and went in on my own. I was ushered up to the third floor and taken to a small room to wait for the consultant, who was seeing another patient. After a short while he appeared round the door, pulled up a chair and sat down opposite me. 'So you think you've got rheumatoid arthritis,' he snapped. This blunt opening almost caused me to break down on the spot. I was tired, I was in pain, I was frightened and no, I did not think I had rheumatoid arthritis, I knew I had rheumatoid arthritis. His manner softened considerably when he had examined me and discovered me to be genuine and in pretty bad condition.

At first he appeared to be rather annoyed that I had discontinued the gold therapy and he kept returning to the subject, although he admitted that it would be unwise to give me any more. He then asked me if I had a good family and neighbours who would look after the children; he wanted me to come into hospital for a few weeks' rest and told me that he feared for my joints in another two years' time if I did not get off them now. I was stunned. I did not give him a final answer but told him that I would have to talk to Stephen and see if I could sort anything out. The thought of being away from the family for several weeks was too awful to contemplate, but I knew I had pushed myself too far in recent months and that more than anything I wanted to collapse into bed and forget all my responsibilities.

I left the building rather gloomily and found Mare who was sitting in the sun reading her latest secondhand book bargain. We sat together for a while watching the pigeons and then set off in a leisurely fashion for home.

6

Stephen met me at Hereford station the next day. We had already spoken on the telephone, so he had had time to absorb the doctor's suggestion. We talked everything over with John from next door, and Tom the churchwarden, and they as doctors both felt that it was imperative that I spend some time resting in hospital.

We telephoned Stephen's mother in Kent and after explaining the situation, asked her if she would be able to come and look after the children for a while. She was delighted to have been asked and agreed to come almost immediately, so rather apprehensively I contacted the hospital in London to tell them that I would be able to stay for some time.

Clare was still a bit young to understand what was happening but I explained to Anna that I needed a rest because my bones were behaving badly and she took it quite calmly and sensibly. I was glad that she had the newness of her school life to occupy her and distract her from the fact that I was going away.

Stephen's mother arrived almost at once and we spent a day going through the general family routine and the moods of the washing machine and the times of 'Playschool' and all the other matters and events to be remembered. She felt confident that she could manage the household and I felt equally confident leaving her in charge.

The day of my departure arrived and I woke up feeling heavy and miserable. We got Anna ready for school and Stephen and I took her down the church path together. We stopped at the school gate and I forced a smile as I kissed her goodbye, but as her little blonde head disappeared through the gate into the playground my feelings overwhelmed me and I turned quickly into the churchyard. She was the youngest child in the school and seemed so vulnerable and small.

It was now time to leave for the station and I could not bear to go through another farewell scene, so I called up the stairs to Clare and Granny; then Stephen closed the front door quickly behind us and we drove away. When we reached the station, Stephen delivered me and my luggage to the right platform for my train to Reading and I insisted that he left and went home. I felt I would be better on my own for a while. I watched him disappear over the bridge and back into the car-park and wondered how I was going to get through the coming weeks. Stephen was to visit me every week, but we had made no plans about the children.

I spent that night with Mare in Pangbourne. The arrangement was that I travel to London the next morning, to be met at Paddington by Wilfrid and Helen. Mare loaded me on to the train and I cowered into a corner seat. I was in a great deal of pain and I was terrified of being tripped over or banged into. We had worked out the route so that I would not have to carry my luggage at any time and that the distance I would have to walk would be minimal, but when we reached Paddington all that was dramatically changed. The train for some reason chose to arrive on a platform some way away from the scheduled platform, where Wilfrid and Helen were waiting for me. I stared at the vast staircases with disbelief and as I had let the crowds surge out of the train before leaving my seat I realised that I had no one to help me carry my bag. I managed to climb down out of the train dragging my bag after me and then I just stood for a while wondering what to do next. With great difficulty I negotiated the bag over my shoulder and set off towards the stairs. How I ever got up them, down the other side and across the length of the station I will never know, but it seemed the longest and most miserable journey I had ever made.

When I reached the other end of the station, the nightmare

11

continued when I realised that no one was there to meet me. Another train had meanwhile come in from Reading and Wilfrid, thinking that I would be on it and not seeing me among the other passengers, assumed that I had fainted or collapsed on the train. He and Helen walked up and down the entire length of the train looking for me and emerged from it looking very worried. We eventually met and fell on each other with relief before making our way to the hospital.

At last we arrived at our destination, and when I checked in, I was handed a large and beautiful bunch of yellow flowers which Stephen had ordered for me. I was taken to a ward which I was to share with another person, and Wilfrid and Helen stayed for a while to help me settle in. My companion was very jolly and cheerful, she quickly drew me out of my gloom and we laughed together a great deal.

Later that afternoon the consultant called in to see me and gave me another examination. He prodded this joint and forced that joint and then peered at me over his spectacles. 'You're a mess,' he said. With these encouraging words he sat down and wrote a list of the treatments I was to have. 'These will do you good,' he said as he left. After a short while a nurse appeared with an assortment of drugs, which I obediently swallowed. In no time at all my head started reeling and I felt very odd indeed. I think I must have slept for a couple of hours. I awoke to find my brother Paul standing by the bed, or rather, several Pauls standing by the bed, as I was still feeling very dizzy. Paul had been installing a computer at a hospital nearby and had found time to call in before returning home to Oxford. I really appreciated the fact that he had visited me, but I was far too fuzzy to take him in properly.

The following days passed in a haze of meals and routine. Once in bed, I realised how thoroughly worn out I was and I marvelled that I had carried on coping for so long. I was thus quite content to lie back and be carried along by hospital routine. Every day the physiotherapist came to put me through an assortment of rituals. A large bowl of hot wax was placed in front of me and I had to put my hands in it until a thick glove of wax formed around them. They were then wrapped in a layer of greaseproof paper and finally covered with a towel. This was repeated on my right knee and when completely parcelled up I would be left like this for about twenty minutes. The sensation of having my hands in hot wax was actually very pleasurable and I quite looked forward to it each day, but therapeutically it had very little value. While my hands and knee were wrapped in wax, my right shoulder received a very different treatment. A large bag of ice was placed on it, secured by a towel and again left there for roughly twenty minutes. When the ice bag was removed, the physiotherapist kneaded and manipulated my shoulder and tried to make me lift it and move it in directions in which it had no intention of going.

After a couple of weeks, the movement had certainly improved but the pain had increased so much in intensity that on occasions I almost screamed. I would wake in the early hours of the morning and find that the only way I could override the pain was to use the breathing exercises that I had learned during pregnancy. I had never found them any use during childbirth but now, strangely enough, I was able to lift myself above the pain even if only for a short time.

I was amazed and flattered by the number of visitors that I received. Word had spread among the St Alban and St Sergius network in and around London, and several friends unexpectedly turned up to see me. My most regular visitors were Wilfrid and Helen, who both taught at colleges quite near to the hospital, Mare, who came to London regularly, and Margaret. One or two friendships were revived when people whom I had not seen for some years came to visit me. In particular I saw a great deal of Anna Georgina, a friend since childhood. She told me that she was getting married the next year and that she wanted to design a dress which she could wear both for her wedding and for playing the harp at concerts. She already had something in mind and asked me if I would like to design the embroidery for her to work on it.

We both decided wild flowers would be a good idea and I promised to start thinking about it when I returned home.

Although I was in bed all the time, the days did not seem long and tedious. There always seemed to be something happening or someone to talk to, even when after the first week I was moved into a room on my own. I slept quite a lot; I read a certain amount and I did quite a bit of embroidery. It hurt my hands and the physiotherapist insisted that I did no more than one hour a day, but I was determined to keep my hands working somehow. My knees became increasingly swollen and painful and, on one occasion, the consultant gave me a steroid injection in my right knee. The relief was immediate, and I temporarily put aside my reservations about having steroids pumped into me. A year earlier I had been given several steroid injections in the tendons in my hands because my fingers would not bend. They had been quite excruciatingly painful, but again the relief came at once.

As the days wore on I met several interesting people in the hospital but I missed Stephen and the children badly. Stephen managed to travel up to London every Thursday to see me, but he was never able to stay for long as he liked to be home to help put the children to bed. Every single night they telephoned me and Anna would tell me with glee each day that she had a new reading book, so I felt secure in the knowledge that she was happy at school. Clare would then tell me what she and Granny had been doing all day.

After two weeks Stephen and his mother quite unexpectedly brought the children to see me. The children were thrilled to travel in both a train and the Underground for the first time and all in one day. I was absolutely amazed when they came clattering up the stairs and they bustled around, very anxious to inspect my room and to see the nurses who were looking after me. They stayed and had some lunch and drew a lot of pictures which I stuck all over my cupboard doors; then sadly Stephen announced that they really ought to be on their way if the children were not to be home too late that evening. To them this visit was new and exciting, almost an adventure, and they left with the prospect of going on yet another train and perhaps even a taxi, but as their voices grew fainter down the stairs, I went back to my room and I sat down and wept. For a while I had survived, but now I had seen Anna and Clare again I just wanted to go home.

As I sat there with my head down, crying, someone came into the room and gently put his hands on my shoulders. It was Hugh, a clergyman whom I had come to know quite well and who had a room on the floor above me. If anyone had tried any 'there, there' talk with me, I would have cried even more, but Hugh's quiet reassuring presence helped to calm me down again. I had met him during the first week when coming out of chapel. He came and chatted to me and my room-mate for some time and we discovered that he had heard my father lecture at a Fellowship conference when I was only two years old. While we talked, I picked up my embroidery and started working on it, and Hugh admired it. He told me that the hospital in Southampton where he was chaplain had just built a new chapel and that it had been dedicated only last June. He had been involved in the design and layout and was now looking for someone to make two embroidered hangings to go on the walls each side of the altar. He described in detail what he had in mind and asked if I might be interested in doing this work for him. I was very flattered and excited to have been asked, but my first re-action was to say 'no'. With two small children and deformed hands, I could see no way in which it would be possible. Hugh told me that if I agreed to do the work I could spend as long as I liked on it and we finally agreed that I would come and look at the chapel before I made a decision.

Hugh went home shortly after Stephen left with the children. He had been coming to say goodbye when he found me crying in my room. We parted with the agreement that I would be in touch when I left hospital.

During the second half of my stay I became restless and I felt unsettled after seeing the children again. Their visit had unsettled them as well and I began to dread their evening phone calls as much as I looked forward to them. Anna no longer told me excitedly about school but asked every night, 'When are you coming home, Mummy? I want you to come home.' Clare was just beginning to form sentences and the first long sentence I ever heard her utter was a pitiful request that she have her mummy back.

I was now feeling extremely sick. The consultant had taken it as a personal affront that I had not responded to gold. 'All my patients get better on gold,' he repeatedly told the staff, and as I had proved to be such a dismal failure he called in another consultant and handed the treatment over to him. This second man prescribed a drug named penicillamine, a last-resort drug, which accumulates in the system and takes weeks, even months, to be effective. For the first week of taking this I was very sick day and night in addition to the dizziness and headaches I was still experiencing from the drug that I had begun to take on my first day in hospital. The severe pain in my right shoulder was increasing and all in all I felt ghastly. After a while the sickness subsided and I was able to eat and sleep again.

When I had completed a month in hospital the doctor told me that he would like me to stay for another three weeks. My heart sank when I heard this. I was enjoying the much needed rest but I want to go home and I knew the family wanted me back too. I was also aware that although Granny was coping admirably she would soon need a break. Stephen came to visit me that day and after discussing it in great detail, we decided that I would go home the following week via Southampton. He was very excited by the idea of the embroidery project and insisted that I go and visit the chapel.

I spent my last week in hospital sleeping, reading, enjoying my visitors and not enjoying the physiotherapy. On two occasions I even ventured outside and walked slowly around the square. Nobody gave me a second glance as I stepped out in my ensemble of duffle coat, nightdress, slippers and walking stick, and as I watched the people dashing from place to place, I noticed with amusement that my own style of dress was not so extraordinary after all.

At the end of the week, a bright day in late October, Wilfrid came to collect me and drove me to Pangbourne. His small son, Edwin, came along for the ride and spent the time crow-spotting as we passed by ploughed fields. Mare had to go out during the afternoon and I was left on my own for a few hours. After some minutes had passed I realised that I was totally disorientated and that I had no idea what to do with myself. For five weeks I had drifted along on someone else's routine; meals and drinks had been brought to me, pills and medicines produced on time, every decision made for me and now, suddenly, I was on my own and it was frightening. I went and knocked on a neighbour's door and sat and talked with her until Mare came home.

The next morning, after a rather stiff and painful start, Mare and I drove to Southampton. Hugh was waiting at the hospital gates for us and he took us at once to the chapel. As we entered I was at once struck by the colour scheme and by the general atmosphere and I sat down to make some notes. Hugh wanted two hangings, one depicting the Annunciation and the other Pentecost, and the three of us discussed how the themes could utilise the colours in the chapel, these being a range of browns, with beige, orange, white and pale blue. Suddenly on impulse I said that I would love to do the work, and Hugh with obvious pleasure told me that I could have as much time as I wanted. I secretly wondered how I would ever manage this seemingly mammoth task but now that I had committed myself I was jolly well going to do it.

As I was anxious to get home to the family, Mare and I bade farewell to Hugh and started our journey back to Lugwardine. We reached home at about four o'clock in the afternoon. When we arrived, the house seemed very quiet. Granny had gone out, Clare was asleep and Stephen was in the kitchen with Anna, who was telling him that he had not made her drink in the way she liked it. They had obviously not heard us arrive, so I walked in quietly and stood at the

47

kitchen door. Suddenly they noticed me, and there were arms flailing in all directions, as we all tried to hug each other at once. The general commotion woke Clare who was carried down sleepily and tearfully and placed in my lap. She said nothing for a while but clung to me tightly like a baby monkey. As if on cue, Granny arrived home almost immediately and we had a very happy reunion at tea-time.

7

Mare had to leave the following morning, but Granny stayed on for a couple of days to make sure that I was going to manage on my own. In spite of everything, I was noticing at this time a calmness, which I would not have expected from myself under such conditions. In fact, with my history of depressive illness, I was surprised that I had not been over-whelmed once again by depression, but I realised that I had not actually been depressed since Clare's birth, neither had I suffered from any nightmares. It was as though the emotion-al problems had receded and evolved into a physical illness.

For about a week I strugged on. I felt rested after my five weeks in hospital, but there was no noticeable improvement in the arthritis. Day by day the rest periods merged into one another, until it became apparent that I was in no fit state to look after a home and two small children. Stephen picked up the telephone and explained the situation to his mother, who was back on our doorstep within forty-eight hours. Once again meals began to appear and washing began to wave around on the line, and for Stephen and the children life became reasonably normal again.

At the beginning of December we received a visit from the clergyman who had anointed me back in July. He was very concerned about my condition and asked if he could again come and anoint me. We fixed a time on the following Friday. This time there was no church service, as I could barely leave my bed; a short service of anointing was carried out by my bedside with just the clergyman, Stephen and myself present. I prayed hard that I would not have the experience of the last time and that now I would really begin to improve. That evening Margaret arrived for a long weekend to look after the children in order to give Granny a rest. She had hoped to arrive in time to be present at the anointing, but in the event had not succeeded.

When I awoke the next day I could neither believe nor understand what had happened to me. Every joint in my body was screaming with such intensity that I could not move any part of me on my own. Stephen and Margaret managed to lever me into a half-sitting position propped up by pillows, where I remained for several hours. If the pillows slipped I slipped with them and could do nothing until someone came and lifted me up again. The pain defies telling, and only a chronic arthritic will ever understand what I was going through. Margaret brought my food to me all cut up like a child's, but I could barely lift it to my mouth, nor move my jaws up and down to eat it. As I lay there motionless for hours on end not even my mind remained active. I was too stunned even to think about the state I was in or about what was going to happen to me. Towards late afternoon I became aware of a violent itching on my cheek and I tried to lift my hand to my face but found it impossible without the help of the other hand. With tears streaming down my face I slowly levered one hand up to my cheek, the whole process taking several minutes and several abortive attempts. When I finally got it there, I found that I could not even apply the necessary pressure, my fingers were so inflamed and painful. At this point I screamed and then began to howl like a wild beast in a trap. The events of the past two years overwhelmed me and I saw I had become a pathetic cripple who could not even scratch her own face. I howled loudly and uncontrollably.

By this time Stephen had come home from visiting in the parish and he came straight upstairs and lay down next to me. I sobbed even harder as I thought about what this sickness must be doing to him and the children. At last, exhausted by pain and crying, I fell asleep.

The following morning brought with it a very slight improvement and I managed, albeit with great difficulty, to go downstairs for a splendid lunch prepared by Granny. I sat on a pile of cushions and had my food cut up for me but it was an achievement of sorts to have come downstairs after the complete immobility of the previous day.

It was when Monday arrived that I was faced with the greatest challenge. That afternoon I had an appointment with the specialist at the hospital and the very thought of having to put on clothes and travel in a car filled me with terror. Margaret and Granny between them were able to get Anna ready for school and look after Clare, so at least I had no worries about the children. Stephen helped me to dress, a slow, awkward, painful business, and then helped me downstairs and into the car. As we drove to the hospital every bump in the road seemed to jolt and jar through my joints and I went into the waiting room feeling very tearful and sorry for myself. Mercifully I did not have to wait long before my name was called and I shuffled into the consulting room and slumped into the chair. This time the specialist did not need to ask me how I was; it was all too obvious. She told me that the time had come for me to accept steroid treatment. I had fought long and hard against this but I was now ready to agree to anything; if she had told me that chopping me into little bits would make me better, I would have agreed to it. Stephen collected the drugs from the pharmacy department and then drove me home. A number of people had collected and were sitting around in the kitchen having tea but I was beyond being sociable and crawled back upstairs and into bed.

That night it began to snow and by morning the snow had settled to quite a depth. Margaret had planned to travel home in the afternoon but we all advised her to set off at once, as we anticipated a slow and rather difficult journey ahead of her. I was sorry to see her go; she had come with the sole intention of helping and giving Granny a bit of a rest, and had quietly and cheerfully done just that.

It continued to snow and was very cold. I felt no incentive

to leave my bed. I had been told that I would feel very different after only a few days on steroids but after a fortnight, I was still not aware of much change. Christmas was approaching, and we urged Stephen's mother to go up to Scotland to spend a few days with his sister and family. Mare would come and stay with us for a while and we would manage as best we could. By now I was able to get up for short periods at a time; perhaps two hours in the morning and then again in the afternoon, but I very quickly tired and my joints complained bitterly at having to support me.

We celebrated Christmas in a very low key fashion. Then Granny returned to us from Scotland, but alas, she had tripped while walking to church at Christmas and had cracked a bone in her ankle. She arrived with a large plaster on her foot but cheerfully insisted that she was still able to cook and look after Clare as long as she could put up her foot in the afternoon. Eventually she had to return home, and I was left to work out the daily time-table which best suited me. Stephen would dress and breakfast the children and see Anna off to school, then I would gradually uncurl and come downstairs. I would prepare a midday meal and then spend the afternoon resting and reading to Clare. By the time Anna came out of school I was able to get up again and meet her and give the children their tea, but very often I did not even have the strength to put them to bed and was myself in bed by about five o'clock.

At about this time, John, our neighbour, asked me if I had considered applying for 'Disabled' stickers to put on my car, so that I could park wherever was convenient for me. I leaped at the idea. My GP signed the appropriate form and a week later I received my assorted orange labels, which I stuck fore and aft of our elderly but much loved Morris Minor. This immediately changed my life and I was able to be completely independent, parking so that I could do the minimum of walking. It also meant that Stephen was not tied by having to drive me, except on the occasions when I really could not manage on my own.

As I was spending so much time resting, I began to get restless and longed to do something creative; although my hands were swollen and painful, I was determined to start using them again. My first commission was to create a design out of wild flowers for Anna Georgina to embroider on her wedding dress. I loved doing this and had many ideas, but I finally settled on a design which I sent off to Anna Georgina. She was delighted with it and began work on the dress almost immediately.

My next assignment was the work that I had promised Hugh, the two hangings depicting the Annunciation and Pentecost. I doodled around on rough pieces of paper for some while and did a certain amount of tearing up and throwing away, but finally I found ideas beginning to shape themselves. I bought some card of the exact dimensions that I intended the finished articles to be and began to transfer the designs. I found drawing on a larger scale rather more difficult, but Sheila patiently modelled Mary while I pencilled, rubbed out and pencilled again. Stephen modelled Gabriel and the characters present at Pentecost. When the designs were completed and the colours in which I intended to embroider them were painted in, we took them down to Southampton for Hugh's approval. He was immediately pleased with them and told me he was very excited at the prospect of the finished work, but he repeated emphatically that I was to take as much time as I needed and not wear myself out working on them.

As the spring advanced, I began to notice an improvement in my condition. The steroids were having some effect and the penicillamine too was beginning to help. Nonetheless I did not feel secure; I felt that this was an artificial improvement and that rather I should be looking for a natural and lasting one. A friend told me how her brother had received a lot of help from a local chiropractor, so I took his name and made an appointment to go and see him. I had never heard of chiropractic and was fascinated at how much this man was able to tell about my condition, past and present, from examining my back. He found that quite a number of vertebrae were misaligned and as he eased them back into place over the following weeks, I began to feel brighter, and certainly the intensity of pain through my shoulders and arms was greatly reduced. He had working with him a nurse named Christine; she and I talked endlessly about all manner of things and I enjoyed my visits very much. The chiropractor also administered herbal medicines, but was reluctant to treat me with herbs while I was taking steroids. I had drawn a blank with the acupuncturist for the same reason; he too felt that he could not achieve anything while I had steroids in my system.

By late spring I returned to the hospital to see the specialist, who told me that she was going to bring me down off the steroids very gradually. Although they were obviously helping me, I was still glad to learn that the dosage was to be lowered. Every month I was able to shed one milligram and there appeared to be no adverse reaction.

Since I had begun to take the penicillamine, I had been testing my urine for protein at regular intervals, and all seemed well until early summer, when quite suddenly the level of protein in the urine became rather high. The specialist told me to reduce the dosage gradually, but as the protein persisted, I had to stop taking the drug altogether. The withdrawal of the penicillamine coincided with the time I came off the steroids altogether and as might be expected my body reacted violently to having both these props taken away simultaneously. As the year wore into autumn and then winter, my condition deteriorated rapidly and I became very gloomy, as the pain increased and my mobility once again decreased. The specialist wrote for advice to my consultant in London, who replied suggesting that I gradually start building up the penicillamine dosage, very slowly to give my body time to adapt it. At this point I became stubborn and refused to take the drug. The level of protein in my urine had not decreased one little bit and I was not prepared to feed into my system something that was clearly not suiting it.

Around Christmas time my whole attitude changed dramatically, sparked off by a chance remark from Anna. On a day when I was obviously unwell, she asked me, 'Mummy, are you going to come to my wedding in a wheel-chair?' Clenching my teeth so that I did not cry, I answered: 'No, I'm going to run down that aisle'. I realised what this illness must be doing to the children and resolved to become the strong, fit and mobile mother that they deserved.

By this time I had almost finished working on the embroideries. I had begun them the previous May and worked intermittently when my gnarled and painful hands would allow. Since they each measured two by three feet, a considerable amount of hard work was involved. As I sewed bit by bit, I began to feel a new sense of my own worth. I was now pretty useless at most things, but it was clear that I could embroider, and embroider well. The appreciative and encouraging remarks from others spurred me on and I was able to finish the two pictures shortly after Christmas.

8

On New Year's day I woke feeling that this year things were going to be different; I was going to get better, or at least begin to. I visited the hospital and told the specialist that one day I was going to be completely well again and that I was going to achieve this without medical treatment. She was pleased that I was so positive, and after taking a blood sample, told me that she would still like to see me regularly to check on my progress. In spite of my determination to fight the disease, the pain raged through me and I took to my bed. Then one morning during January the specialist rang me from the hospital; she had just received the result from my blood test and was very much concerned. The activity was rapidly rising and was heading for the level that it had reached a year earlier, when I had been completely crippled. 'Mrs Parsons,' she said, 'I really must insist that you start taking the penicillamine again.' As I put the telephone down, I felt sick. This was not supposed to be happening; I was supposed to be getting better. The protein level had still not shifted, but I wondered if I had any alternative but to take the drug.

That week I had an appointment with the chiropractor, who was still treating me periodically, and he and Christine were worried to see me so despondent. Christine handed me a piece of paper that she had been keeping for me and on it was the name Peter Scothern. She explained that he was an itinerant healing evangelist and that he came regularly to Hereford and held meetings in the Shire Hall. A friend of hers who had been dying of cancer had received the laying-on-of-hands regularly at these meetings and was now completely healed. I went home and discussed it with Stephen; we remembered having seen his name in the paper some time before. Stephen had made various enquiries about him then, but as he had learned nothing we had abandoned the interest. Now I was prepared to revive the interest, particularly as I felt disappointed in my search for healing within my own tradition of the Anglican Church. Peter Scothern was next due in Hereford on the following Wednesday, but Stephen, because of another meeting, was not able to come with me. I contacted Christine to ask her if she would accompany me, and she at once agreed. I also mentioned the meeting to Rachel, a friend in the village, who expressed interest and asked if she could come along with us. I felt rather apprehensive as the day approached. Because of my High Church background, I had always been slightly suspicious of charismatics. This, I readily confess, was fear based on ignorance.

Wednesday dawned, and as I related at the beginning of this story, Anna climbed into our bed and uttered her prophecy. Stephen and I looked at each other in amazement, but we said nothing. I spent a part of the day resting to preserve my strength for the evening and then when the children were in bed and the baby-sitter comfortably established, I set out to collect Rachel and Christine. It was cold and drizzly when we reached the Shire Hall, and we were glad to get into the warmth of the building. We found ourselves faced with many doors and passages, but we followed the sound of cheerful chatter and were virtually pulled into the room by welcoming handshakes and inviting smiles. A few people had already assembled and were dotted around the room or standing talking in huddles. We sat down somewhere in the middle on those institutional canvas chairs that make you itch if you sit on them for too long.

Very quickly the room filled to capacity and a man who was sitting with a group of others at a table facing us, stood up and suggested that we start singing some choruses. A portable organ wheezed into action, a few people banged their tambourines and everyone began to sing lustily. I did not recognise any of the tunes and I found it far too noisy, but I was struck by the fervour with which the people around me were singing.

After a while the singing ceased and three men seated at the table stood up in succession, first to give out notices and then to read from the Bible. When the readings were finished, a Welsh woman stood up to give a testimony of her healing. She told us how nine years earlier she had been completely crippled by multiple sclerosis and at the time had received the laying-on-of-hands from Peter Scothern. Eighteen months later, there was no trace of the disease in her body and to this day she is strong and healthy. Her testimony was followed by more singing and a number of people began to speak in tongues. The atmosphere was one of great fellowship and I would stress that there was no whipping-up of emotion.

At last Peter Scothern got to his feet and began speaking. He spoke to us gently and simply, with none of the shouting and hell fire that I had previously been led to expect. I liked his approach. It was a refreshing contrast to the indecipherable theology that I had known as a child. I do not clearly remember everything that he said on that evening, but the impact that it had on me was tremendous. Finally Peter asked us all to stand and sing a hymn and invited those of us who wanted healing or were troubled in any way, to come to the front for a blessing. I went forward with a few others and we formed a semi-circle around him. He came to us all in turn, talking briefly with each person and then praying with them. As he stood in front of me I told him that I had rheumatoid arthritis, and he asked me if I believed that God could heal me. I answered 'yes', without being fully convinced, and he placed his hands on my head and in the name of Christ commanded the infirmity to leave me. As he prayed I felt a hazy dizzy feeling, which spread through my body, and I fell to the floor. Strong arms behind me caught me and lowered me gently down so that I did not hurt myself and I was struck by how little pain I felt. A fall in normal circumstances would have set me screaming. Rachel told me afterwards that she had rushed forward when I fell, thinking that something dreadful had happened to me, but was assured by everyone around us that I was perfectly all right.

By the time that I had been helped to my feet, the meeting was almost at an end. Christine, Rachel and I left the building, feeling moved and dazed by the experience and we drove home more or less in silence. Stephen heard the car and came out to greet me. Naturally he wanted to know everything about the meeting, but I felt unable to communicate very much and I was extremely tired. I crawled up to bed and tried to sleep but my mind seemed to be whirling uncontrollably. I found myself beginning to cry gently and then hysterically, but I was not able to tell Stephen why; I did not even know myself. At last in the early hours I fell asleep, but woke almost immediately, remembering that I had left a casserole cooking in the Aga since the previous midday. I went downstairs to the kitchen and took the charred remains of the meal out of the oven. As I surveyed the wreckage I once again broke down and cried and began to throw things around the kitchen because I was so angry with myself. I went back upstairs and threw a pair of shoes across the bedroom before climbing into bed; then I wept for a further two hours before finally falling asleep.

When morning came, I woke utterly exhausted, but I felt cleansed and completely at peace. As the following days passed I noticed a quite striking difference in my physical condition. It appeared that the disease, which had so recently raged furiously through my body, had taken an about-turn and was retreating. I found myself accepting with calmness that my healing had begun, but I also accepted realistically that such great damage had been done to my body that the healing process would inevitably happen over a period of time.

At about this time I had an appointment with a homoeopath. In spite of my belief that I was recovering, I kept the appointment and explained to the homoeopath that

I knew I was getting better and why. He was entirely in sympathy with my belief and told me he would like to treat me nevertheless, to help strengthen my body and its own capacity to heal. He examined me thoroughly and asked me a number of questions before deciding which treatment to give me. I visited him three or four times over the next few months and he expressed delight at the pace at which I was improving.

I visited the hospital twice during the spring. My blood test showed that the activity of the disease was rapidly declining and by late May a further test showed the viscosity level to be within normal limits. As far as I was concerned, the disease was dying, and now I could concentrate on seeing the extensive joint damage gradually healing itself.

Sheila remarked one day that she was amazed how much better I was looking and how wonderful it was that the penicillamine had begun working so rapidly. I smiled and told her that I had not swallowed a single drug for months. She seemed taken aback by this revelation, but was interestedly, reservedly, when I explained to her something of the healing ministry of Peter Scothern.

As my strength increased, I began to think that perhaps I could manage without the regular home help visits. I rang their office and explained that I would still be having help from one of our parishioners, so that they would not think I was being rash by trying to cope alone. The home help supervisor told me that they would always be there if I needed them and I assured her that I believed I would never need them again.

During June our annual Petertide festival came round once again, with our newly-formed tradition of holding a concert in the church. On this occasion we invited Anna Georgina, recently married, to come to play the harp and sing for us. She had married Keith in April, and we had all managed the journey to London to be present at the wedding. I felt very proud to see the embroidery, which I had designed and Anna Georgina had so beautifully executed, walking up the aisle.

She wore the same dress to the concert and gave us an evening of music that was talked about long afterwards in Lugwardine. Anna wandered around for days with a glazed expression and decided from then on that her life's ambition was to play the harp like Anna Georgina.

I had now experienced five consecutive months of improvement, but with the advent of July my condition was to worsen considerably. The weather was unbearably hot, which in itself was no help to any arthritic, but my pain was something beyond that which climatic conditions could cause.

A week later came a blow, with which, even as I write, I have not yet fully come to terms. At Easter Baljeet had telephoned to tell me that she would soon be having major heart surgery in London. Remembering that our lives had so often run parallel, I told her how much better I was and we tentatively arranged that she would come and stay in Hereford to convalesce. Then one Sunday morning early in July, just as I was leaving the house to go over to church, the telephone rang. The front door was open and I could barely hear the voice at the other end above the noise of the church bells, but I recognised it as that of her eldest sister and I guessed at once what she had to tell me. Baljeet had died some hours after the operation two days before. I collapsed in a heap at the bottom of the stairs in a wave of tears and disbelief; then with the worst timing in the world, the doorbell rang and I looked up to see a tramp standing on the step, hungry and expectant. His expression showed that he demanded an explanation for my tear-stained face and as I sobbed out the story he touched me gently on the arm to comfort me.

Baljeet's funeral was to be on the following day in London. Tom and his wife Jess agreed to look after Anna and see her to school in the morning, while Stephen, Clare and I travelled to London. The crematorium was packed to capacity with Indians and the service was conducted both in Punjabi and Gujerati, the respective languages of Baljeet and her husband. The occasion was fraught with emotion and my re-union with her family was a sad one. Their loss was the greater, but I felt that a part of me had gone with Baljeet. I remember the final words of the service which were spoken in English, 'in heaven and in peace', and I take comfort in my belief that death is the ultimate healer.

9

The summer wore on and my joints continued to hurt. Then one day Stephen saw something in a magazine which began to lift my spirits a little. An organisation called Arthritis Care, sponsored by a drug company, was running an award scheme for arthritics under the age of thirty-five. The awards were being offered regionally for achievements in various fields, and Stephen and I felt that I should enter photographs of the two embroideries that I had made under difficult conditions. Tom agreed to sponsor me and we contacted Hugh, who chivvied the photographic department in the hospital into producing the prints as soon as possible. The photographs were perfect in every respect, and many people who have looked at them framed under glass, have asked if they are looking at the actual embroideries, not realising that they are considerably reduced in size. Tom and Hugh wrote embarrassingly flattering accounts of my battle with illness and my determination to make the embroideries, and I sent these off with the photographs. Some weeks passed; then one morning in the autumn I received a letter announcing that I had won an award as a runner-up in my area, which appeared to cover the Midlands and East Anglia. The letter gave details of when and where the awards were being presented, and a few weeks later we all travelled to London.

In all there were eighteen of us, ranging in age from twelve to thirty-five. As I looked around the room and listened to the various conversations, I found myself biting back the tears. Virtually everyone there had been arthritic since childhood, and all of them had stories to tell of drug damage and growth stunted through the excessive use of steroids. A child of twelve already had artificial joints. Although I had myself gone through a period of crippling pain and disability, I knew the worst was now in the past for me, and I was looking towards the day when I would forget I had ever been an arthritic. I looked around at these other people, for whom it was all very much in the present, and I felt sick and disgusted to see what the disease and its treatment can do to a life.

Stephen and the children came to collect me and the children were bursting with excitement over what they had seen and done. I listened appreciatively but the events of the day had left me subdued and unconversational.

By now the autumn term was well under way. Anna had moved up a class and also started piano lessons. These she loved; she worked hard and practised enthusiastically. Clare, who had been attending the new playgroup in the village, decided that she did not want to go any more. She was due to begin school on a part time basis after Christmas and since I enjoyed her company and she was very good at amusing herself, I did not press on her any suggestion of going back to the playgroup.

At this time of the year it was customary for the local Oxford Society, of which Stephen is a member, to hold a dinner for members, spouses and friends. Stephen and I were able to attend this time and we arrived at the chosen place and began to talk with a few people who had already gathered. Suddenly I became aware of a rather severe woman watching me from the other side of the room and after a while, I began to feel uncomfortable. At length the woman crossed the room and came towards me. She asked me about my stick and I told her a little bit about my illness. Still looking rather severe she looked me directly in the eyes and said, 'One day you will be able to help others more than you could ever realise.' I remember blushing bright red as she turned and disappeared back into the crowd. The rest of the evening passed in a haze of good food and pleasant company; when the time came to leave, there she was again, standing by the exit door. She took my hand, kissed me on the cheek and said, 'Remember what I've told you.'

Shortly after this Stephen attended a conference and Anna's godmother, Helen, came to stay with me while he was away. Helen played the violin and with me on the recorder, we had often played simple medieval music together. On this occasion we had the idea of giving a small concert, which we could perform at the primary school. The head teacher was delighted with the idea and so for an entire day we rehearsed a number of pieces. I was quite out of practice at first, after being unable to play for so long, but gradually my fingers began to move as I commanded them. When we considered ourselves to be reasonably well rehearsed, we went across to the school, and the children all assembled in the hall. Clare went and sat on the floor with Anna, clearly pleased to feel that she was one of the school children. Helen and I talked to the children about the instruments and the music that we were going to play and about the people who would originally have enjoyed it. Then we played and sang a number of pieces. They enjoyed listening as much we enjoyed playing and the head teacher asked me if I would like to come into school regularly, to listen to the recorder players and perhaps help to polish up their technique. She commented that she remembered a time, not so long ago, when I would barely have been able to pick up a recorder, let alone to play it.

It was while Helen was staying that a very exciting thing happened. Two years previously I had taken off my wedding ring, because of the swelling and deformity in my hands, and I had believed that I would never be able to wear it again. After playing the recorder and finding that my fingers were becoming more agile, I studied my hands and saw that the swelling and deformity had noticeably subsided over the past few months. I took the wedding ring from the chain round my neck and tried to slide it on to my finger. It fitted with no argument, and Helen and I threw our arms round each other for joy. This was a major milestone and I could not wait to show Stephen.

At the end of the week I drove Helen home to Oxford and collected Stephen. He was thrilled when I showed him my left hand with the wedding ring once again in its correct place; then he told me *his* exciting news. He had been approached by an editor of a religious publishing house, who had heard indirectly about my experience of healing. He was asked whether he knew anyone who could write a critical but sympathetic survey of the Christian healing ministry in this country. So much was going on in so many places and in so many different ways that there was a need for someone to draw the threads together and to try to see the inherent unity running through the different approaches. Although Stephen was not actually asked to do this work, he felt that this expressed need was a challenge to which he wanted to respond, and shortly afterwards he wrote off to ask whether it was in order for him to tackle the project himself. He realised that it would involve much travel, field work and correspondence. Gradually, after many letters had been written, he was able to arrange interviews with a wide variety of people with an interest in the healing ministry all over the country.

Before Stephen began on his frequent trips up and down the country, we learned of three American healing evangelists who were touring Wales. Stephen found that he was free on the evening that Jim Sepulveda, one of the three, was holding a meeting at Mountain Ash. As we had heard something of his remarkable reputation, we were eager to hear him speak.

As we drove along the road at the head of the Welsh valleys, the sun was setting in long low orange streaks and the lights in the mining towns below us began to twinkle as the sky darkened. It was new territory for both of us and we felt in more than one sense as though we were going on an adventure. It was dark when we arrived in Mountain Ash and the town appeared on first impression to be indistinguishable from the others through which we had passed. We arrived at the chapel just as the drizzle began to fall lightly, and were greeted at the door by two men. As I stood shivering, one of them guided me towards the door and said, 'Come in, it's hotting up in there.' 'Spiritually?' Stephen asked. 'Yes, that too,' laughed the man. We found empty seats at one side of the chapel and sat down. Jim Sepulveda was late, and the congregation were singing to pass the time as they waited for him. They were a complete cross-section of age groups and quite near to us were sitting a large number of children, mostly boys.

At length Jim walked into the chapel and made his way unobtrusively towards the front. The atmosphere was expectant as he began to speak. His message was one of powerful simplicity, and his speech, like Peter Scothern's, was completely free of jargon and came directly from the heart. After a while I began to feel that I was in the presence of a very great and enveloping love. When he had spoken for about forty minutes, he invited people to come forward for healing, and as my own progress had slowed down considerably during the summer, I stood up and walked down towards where he was standing. I told him that my healing had begun earlier in the year but had now come to a standstill and that I was in need of fresh encouragement.

Jim began to speak to me but I barely heard what he said. At the same moment he touched me lightly on the hand and immediately I felt myself falling as a mild electric shock sensation surged through my body. This happened so quickly and unexpectedly that there was no one near to catch me, and Jim himself caught the full weight of my body as I fell forward on to the floor. Several other people came up for a blessing, including the row of young boys, who had sat still and attentive throughout the meeting so far. When everyone had returned to their seats, Jim turned to face the congregation, and after looking round briefly, he told us that there were three people present with back problems and he described in detail their symptoms. After a bit of coaxing, the three people stood up and he prayed for their healing. He then described several other illnesses and occasionally pointed directly at a person and asked him or her to come forward. One by one, all those who had been too shy to ask for healing came forward in amazement and stood in front of him to receive a blessing.

At one point he looked directly at me and said 'You with the blue jersey, come down here.' I was very puzzled by this, as I had already been to him once but I obediently walked forward and stood in front of him again. He looked at me for a few moments and then said, 'I don't really know why I've called you here but I can see the aura of the Holy Spirit around you. I think God is trying to say something to you. He wants to tell you that it comes from God and not from man.' Again he touched my hand and although I was trying to concentrate on what he was still saying to me, I felt myself falling and briefly entered oblivion and complete peace. I puzzled for months over his words, but the peace has remained with me in some measure since that night, and I know that it continues at all times to give me a greater sense of the presence of God.

I grew gradually stronger. Often I felt that my progress was negligible and I was always aware of how much further I had to go, but I would try to balance this by reminding myself from what depths I had already risen. Other people perhaps noticed my continuing improvement more than I did myself. I was still in pain, though of a much lesser intensity than before, and this probably clouded my own vision, whereas others looking at me objectively and not experiencing the pain could observe my ever increasing mobility and stamina. As the year grew colder, I prepared myself for the seasonal barrage of remarks linking the weather with my condition. 'No,' I have told enquirers over and over again, 'the cold weather does not have a bad effect on my joints.'

The build-up to Christmas was now upon us, and I was approached by Anna's head teacher, who asked me to sort out the musical side of the school Christmas concert. For once I was able to make a commitment, knowing that I could fulfil it without deteriorating mid-way and crawling back to bed for a week. I chose the music, organised the different instrumentalists, mainly recorders but with me on the crumhorn, and managed to attend every single rehearsal without difficulty. In fact I was impressed by my own strength, and with the accompaniment of Tom on the piano, I thoroughly enjoyed every moment, in spite of the near-freezing temperature in the church.

After Christmas Clare began school. She immediately settled in and made reading her priority in life, running excitedly down the church path each day to show me her latest reading book. I worried at first that she would not socialise because of her shyness, but she quickly made friends and appeared to be very happy. At about this time I once again felt my progress to be flagging and I suspected that this was a blockage within me, a spiritual blockage rather than a physical one. I knew that my healing was a process; not a purely physical improvement but a gradual disclosure of God and the maturing of my relationship with him. Through prayer I experienced this realisation, but inevitably there were the periods of emptiness, or the 'dark night of the soul'.

It was during one of these periods that I wandered into church one day, wondering and asking what I had to do to raise myself out of the rut into which I had temporarily fallen. I thought that my question was not being answered, but as I turned to leave the church, the words rang clearly through my head, 'Write down your experiences; write a book that will encourage other people.' My first reaction was a negative one – 'Other people in my family write books, not me' – but that evening I sat down and started to write. I even found that I enjoyed it and the most remarkable thing was that the more I wrote, the faster my physical condition improved. By the end of a month, after my initial burst of writing, the difference in my mobility and level of pain was quite extraordinary. When I told Peter Scothern about this on his next visit to Hereford, he pounced on me during the evening meeting and asked me to bring everyone up-to-date with my progress. At first my shyness made me refuse, but then feeling this to be a bit churlish, I stood up and spoke, mentioning in particular my writing and the subsequent rapid continuation of physical healing. I was very much touched by the way in which those present were always so ready to share another person's joys and achievements and to offer further encouragement.

I had with me that evening two friends, one of them an elderly woman named Joyce, who suffered from arthritis and numerous other complaints. She made it quite clear that she did not like the meeting, although she much enjoyed listening to Peter speaking. After the meeting I helped my two friends into the car. Suddenly I heard a voice inside me saying, 'Run.' I argued with it but again it ordered, 'Run.' Before I realised what was happening, I found myself running full pelt around the car park, leaping over puddles and jumping in the air. It seemed the most natural thing in the world and I momentarily forgot the pain and the years of being crippled. After a few minutes I knew I had to stop. There had been no fundamental change in the condition of my joints and I did not want to cause any further damage. As I climbed into the car, Joyce said to me, 'What were you doing, Frances? You are a show-off.' I just smiled and drove her home. The next Sunday she came up to me after church and said, 'I am sorry I called you a show-off but I didn't know how to react. I really believe I saw a miracle that night.' She told a number of people about the incident, and Stephen and I both noticed a softening in her general attitude. She died a few weeks later, and I believe that she died with a measure of healing, through having witnessed and acknowledged a miracle.

I have no doubt that someone of a cynical nature would attribute my running on that night to some form of hysteria, a common criticism of charismatic meetings.

In fact I had been rather detached throughout the evening, as I was particularly tired, and I had not gone forward for the laying-on-of-hands. It would be difficult to be overcome with hysteria in a cold damp car park, when exhausted and anxious to go home. As I write, it is some time since that night and I cannot run, but I see that incident as a 'gift of hope' and an encouragement to look forward.

10

One Saturday morning in May I received a letter from a friend called Juliet. She was in a hospital in London, awaiting major surgery. She had told me some time before that she had been diagnosed as having a congenital hip deformity and that this had remained undetected until she was thirty-one, by which time considerable damage had been caused. She wrote that she was going to have surgery on the following Thursday and asked us to pray for her. I sat up in bed and said, 'I'm going to see her'. I packed nightdresses and toothbrushes and bundled the children into the car; by twelve o'clock, we had reached Mare's house. She was happy to look after the children during the afternoon, so after a quick lunch, the three of them left me at Reading station.

I suddenly felt very vulnerable; this was to be my first journey entirely on my own for some years and I had quite lost the habit of being independent. I managed the steps and the train with no difficulty but on reaching Paddington I took a taxi, realising that the tube was a little beyond my capabilities. The taxi-driver took me right up to the entrance of the hospital, and I climbed out and gazed at the vast building and wondered how many miles of corridor I would have to conquer before I found Juliet. I eventually did find her on the ninth floor. She was in a bed at the far corner of the ward, looking out over the roof tops of London. As I crossed the ward she looked up and the expression on her face is one that I shall long treasure. It was one of utter amazement, mixed with delight. We had not seen each other for some while and as far as Juliet knew, I was still completely crippled. I told her that the purpose of my visit was twofold.

First, I wanted to give her some encouragement by showing her what I had achieved and how I had achieved it; secondly I wanted, for the sake of my own pride, to see how much I was capable of. We talked for about an hour and she told me she was much more confident about her coming operation, now that she had seen my own remarkable recovery. Obviously I could make no claims on her behalf, but I could encourage her through example.

Stephen's research was by now well under way, and he was travelling all over the country, interviewing a number of people involved with healing. After a time, we found that the most amazing coincidences were happening. The right information would fall into his lap at a crucial moment, or the right person would write or telephone with uncanny timing. These incidents occurred so often that Stephen felt that he was being caught up in a process larger than himself. The people whom he interviewed received him with enormous generosity, and he was amazed to discover that in spite of their considerable reputations in some cases, these healers had never before been interviewed in depth about their work.

One evening in April, in his capacity as Ecumenical Officer, Stephen attended a dinner organised by the Full Gospel Business Men's International. By chance he found himself sitting next to the speaker, an American named Don Martin. He was over in England with Jim Sepulveda, and the two of them were holding meetings throughout Wales and the West Midlands. Stephen told him about his research and Don was very willing to be interviewed. It was arranged that Stephen should contact him when he and Jim were together in Alsager, a small town near Stoke-on-Trent. Up till this time I had not accompanied Stephen on any of his interviews, but this time I was anxious to go with him, as I particularly wanted to meet Jim Sepulveda personally. On the appointed day Stephen and I set out early and drove as fast as our elderly vehicle would allow, to be in time for the appointment. We received a warm welcome and spent the hour before lunch with Don, who obviously enjoyed talking and had plenty to say.

Jim was a much quieter person and kept himself in the background until the afternoon, when he opened up and spoke to us at length about his healing ministry. He had been very silent during lunch, but he revealed that while listening to me answering questions about my illness, God had told him to pray for me and my continuing recovery. He signalled to me to get up out of my chair. We stood opposite each other at different ends of the small sitting room and Jim began to speak. He raised his hand as if making a sign of the cross in the air, and immediately, though several feet away from him, I experienced the same mild but beautiful electric shock coursing through my body, and I fell back into Stephen's arms. Jim continued to pray for some time; at intervals he would say 'the anointing is still upon you, I can see it,' and he would pray further. It was as though he was transferring a physical radiance from himself to me. I did not really understand what was happening, but I was certainly conscious of a tremendous power of peace, which had nothing to do with any kind of emotional uplift.

At length I climbed unsteadily to my feet, and Jim came over to me and gave me a warm embrace. Then as he turned to leave the room he stopped, looked at the floor and then at me. 'I want you to go to your friend,' he said, 'and place your hands on her hip and pray for her healing.' I had told the two men about Juliet, and about how she was having surgery on that very afternoon, and we had prayed for her earlier. At first I was taken aback, but almost immediately I remembered the importance of obedience. As we went through the door, I told him that I felt confident about Juliet. He smiled enigmatically and said, 'So do I.' There was something about this man and the aura of his personality which could only be described as tangible holiness. Stephen and I drove home, feeling otherworldly, and we barely noticed the heat and the motorway traffic.

The following week was the school half-term, so we were

able to travel to London and visit Juliet. The children were fascinated by the long hospital corridors and the enchanting painted tiles depicting nursery rhymes and fairy tales, and then of course by the lift up to the ninth floor. I went into the ward alone at first, to ask the sister if I could bring the children in. I explained that they were used to their own mother wobbling around on a stick and would be very careful in a ward where a number of patients were on crutches. She agreed without question and showed us into a side-room where Juliet was now on her own.

Juliet was lying in bed, looking tired but contented. She was surprised to see me again so soon and very pleased to see Stephen and the children after a gap of two or three years. Anna and Clare positioned themselves at the window to absorb the view, while we talked to Juliet and learned about her operation. The surgeon had broken her hip and remoulded it and she was now in traction, eight pounds on each leg for a whole month while the bones knitted together. She told us that the doctor would keep an eye on the hip for ten months or so and then operate on the other one. This would mean having one leg shorter than the other for several months and the inevitable uncertainty of not knowing when she would be summoned back into hospital.

After a while I told Juliet about Jim Sepulveda and about how he had instructed me to come and lay hands on her. Her immediate reaction was positive and she was keen that I should do so. At this point I turned to Stephen. I had not really discussed it with him, perhaps through shyness, because I had no experience of praying with other people; but now it seemed entirely right that I ask him to pray while I laid hands on Juliet. I went round to the other side of the bed and placed my hands on the bandaged area of her left hip, while Stephen began to pray for her healing. Almost at once I was aware that something was happening. The area beneath my hands was moving around with a definite but gentle turbulence, like rice pudding just below the boil, and rather than being puzzled or surprised, I found myself believing with a calm acceptance that the hip was being healed, and at that very moment. I said nothing of this to Juliet, but she volunteered the information that a fuzzy tingling sensation had shot the length of her leg and that she had never experienced this particular feeling before. We became aware of a nurse hovering in the doorway and as Juliet was obviously tired, we left her, she promising to write to us with news of her progress.

The children were thirsty and hungry by this time, so we sat in the visitors' canteen, which was furnished with cheerful plants. While the children were absorbed in their food and surroundings, I told Stephen about the movement I had felt in Juliet's hip. His reaction was much as mine had been at the time. He was not surprised, neither did he challenge me; but quietly accepted, as I had done, that God had intervened and that the hip was being healed.

A month passed and we began to watch the post, knowing that Juliet would soon be taken off traction. At last a letter arrived and I eagerly tore it open. Juliet reported that the doctor was so delighted with her progress that he planned to operate on the other hip within the next month. She also wrote that when standing with her full weight on the left hip she felt absolutely no pain. At first I wanted to cry with happiness – this was the news I had expected – but then gradually I found a loss of confidence creeping in. If the hip had been healed as I believed it had, why was she on crutches? Why did she need them? Was I expecting too great a degree of healing? I began to feel confused.

I decided to go up to London and visit Juliet again. I rang the sister on her ward to ask if I might visit out of hours because of the distances involved and she replied: 'Yes, certainly, but you will find Juliet a bit groggy; we've just done the other hip.' 'What?' I exploded. This was exactly five weeks after the first operation; I could hardly believe my ears. I arranged for the children to be out of school the following day; we took the train to London the next morning and arrived at the hospital shortly before midday. Juliet had been moved back into the main ward and was sitting up in bed looking thinner and obviously tired but wearing the same wide grin that is so much a part of her personality.

The children again parked themselves at the window and I sat down at the bedside. At first I asked Juliet general questions about her hip and she repeated the tale of how amazed the doctors had been by her progress. Then I felt bold enough to ask her if she attached any significance to this and she immediately answered, 'Oh yes, I had no doubt in my mind when you left me last month that I was going to be healed.' This excited me tremendously, for I had wanted the claim to come directly from her and not from me. She went on to tell me more details. When she was first taken off traction, the consultant explained that he was going to manipulate her hip to find out how much movement there was. This he did and was amazed that Juliet was not feeling any pain. He then asked her to lift her leg off the bed, warning her that she might only manage an inch or two. She shot her leg right up in the air and in her own words, 'The consultant's eyes shot out on stalks.' It was then that he decided to operate straight away on the other hip and in the event Juliet had been given less that forty-eight hours advance warning.

Ever since Stephen and I had prayed with Juliet, we had wondered whether we had been in some way transferring a power from Jim Sepulveda, or whether God was indicating that we as a pair were to have a healing ministry of our own. Had Jim been given some indication of this? Whatever the truth was, we believed that it would be revealed to us in time.

11

For some weeks after the Juliet incident we continued to revel in the wonder of what had happened and Juliet's infrequent but welcome letters assured us that all was continuing well and that she would soon be leaving hospital. In the early autumn she returned home and began to attend a local hospital for daily physiotherapy.

At about this time I was approached one Sunday morning by a member of the congregation, a woman I barely knew, named Beth. 'You are looking so much better,' she said. 'What have you been doing?' I told her briefly about the events of the previous year or so and she listened with great interest and then told me about her son, Richard. Now twenty-one years old, he had been suffering from ulcerative colitis since his mid-teens and had recently been in hospital after a particularly nasty flare-up of symptoms. 'We've tried everything,' she told me. 'I wish you could talk to him and give him some hope.' I told her that I would willingly see him if he wanted me to and in less than a week she telephoned me to say that he would be home at the weekend and was anxious to talk to me.

He arrived on our doorstep on the Saturday afternoon, pale and thin. I ushered him in wondering how I was to begin but in no time at all two hours had passed. Stephen came in and after we had talked further it seemed natural that we offer to pray with Richard. We took him over to the church and together laid hands on him and prayed. He was visibly moved, but unable to express very much and I watched him walk down the hill slowly with his head bowed. The next day during Evensong I looked up towards the altar during the intercessions and saw in the place where Richard had been kneeling a thin outline of light. I closed my eyes and opened them again but the light had gone in an instant like the tail end of a rainbow.

Richard came to see us regularly for some months and the most striking and immediate change in him was the complete reorientation of his ideas and relationships. The physical change unfolded gradually and by Christmas, not only had the persistent rectal bleeding of some years standing ceased, but Richard had also weaned himself off the high steroid dose on which he had been, and was maintaining the improvement on a low dosage. His hospital specialist expressed surprise and delight at Richard's recovery and offered to take him into hospital, in order to run tests to find out how this wonderful change had come about. Richard refused. During the early spring Richard telephoned his mother and reported that his boss had recently stopped and questioned him. 'Are we giving you too much work to do? You always seem to be running around.' 'It's so great to feel well again, Mum,' he laughed. 'I just want to run all the time.' Richard's steady recovery and change at all levels of his person gave us confidence with the others who were now beginning to come to us for help.

After some months Stephen and I realised that we were being guided along a graded course and that we were never being presented with a situation that we could not handle. Each person who came to us would help us towards a new insight, which in turn would be vital and relevant for the next person, and so on. This continues to be the case today, and we always stress during counselling that we are as much in a learning as a teaching position.

The thing that has become increasingly clear to us as we pray with people is how often prayer can project individuals into a totally new orbit of concern. They come to us burdened with physical illness and accompanying emotional and spiritual problems. Prayer seems to have the effect of shifting the burden dimension of the illness and even when the illness is apparently not removed, their attitude to it is changed. They become aware of a new process at work in the situation, that is, the will of God for their lives. Knowing in a wonderful way that there is a direction, a path for them to tread, is a cause of happiness and exhilarating freedom. They perceive for themselves the priorities that they must pursue, and we stand back amazed and grateful for the change that the touch of God through prayer has made to the life of each individual.

A wonderful example of this can be illustrated by Jane, a woman beset by problems enough to crush a weaker spirit. When we first met and prayed with her, she was suffering from a debilitating disease of the lungs, which left her weak and breathless. In addition to this, she was closely involved with the problems of her daughter and a criminal son-in-law, from whom she received constant abuse and lack of co-operation. Over a period of time, during which we prayed with her on a number of occasions, we watched her whole command of the situation transform into one of quiet confidence and simple trust that God was in control. Previously, in times of great stress, her physical condition had sent her to hospital for a period, but she now confirmed that her new found peace would override the anxiety that had formerly brought on a crippling attack.

We find constantly that the easiest to help are those who will acknowledge their need for help, a need which is often recognised subsequently as a need of God. Sadly there are many who will not realise this need, until they are brought low through sickness, pain or despair. I fully admit that I did not seriously look for healing until I had reached the bottom both physically and spiritually, but paradoxically how blessed I was to be in that position where I could receive what I have subsequently received.

I once felt a dismal failure over a parishioner, who was a fellow-arthritic. I found that all my attempts at concern and suggestions of help for her were being thrown back in my face and she would repeatedly tell me, 'I'm a very strong person, I don't need help.' I now realise that the failure was not necessarily mine and that no one can help her until she can confess her need. The New English Bible sensitively translates the first of the Beatitudes as 'Blessed are they who know their need of God.' By Christmas of 1984 we had prayed with several people, and the outcome in each case gave us sufficient confidence to continued in this ministry.

As the end of the year approached, Anna, faithful to her earlier desire to study the harp, was now agitating that we find her a teacher. Within a few weeks she herself had found one, and after this everything seemed to fall into place. Anna Georgina offered us the loan of a Celtic harp that she was housing for a friend and he subsequently agreed to sell it to us, when it became clear that Anna was both serious and talented.

Shortly after Christmas the area was swept by a particularly vicious influenza and people were dropping like flies. By February it had reached us. Stephen recovered swiftly, but I was laid low for a month. As everyone knows, 'flu will always attack one's weaknesses and in my case it was my bones. All the progress I had made in the previous year and all the strength I had built up were cancelled out. I felt betrayed.

During the spring we received the news that Clare was to be admitted to hospital in London to have her tonsils and adenoids removed. For almost a year she had suffered from enlarged tonsils and her ears were frequently inflamed. She was generally very miserable and was missing school intermittently. We opted for a London hospital, as our GP found that waiting lists there were only a month compared with local waiting lists of well over a year.

Clare and I travelled to London in Holy Week. After various preliminaries such as hearing and blood tests, the registrar who was to operate told me that one of her ears was badly glued up and that he would have to insert a grommet. This would mean no swimming for two years and possibly several journeys to London for check-ups. I was not very happy about this but accepted it as inevitable if it would help Clare. That evening the anaesthetist visited all her patients for the following day's operating list and I was puzzled when she left the ward without speaking to us. Shortly afterwards a nurse informed me, somewhat casually, that Clare's haemoglobin count was so low that it would not be safe to anaesthetise her. I was devastated and spent a sleepless night worrying about Clare's blood and wondering how I was going to break to her the news that she would not be having the operation for which she was all keyed up and prepared.

The following morning a young doctor asked if he could take some more of Clare's blood. By now she was tired of being poked and prodded and she made it none too easy for him. We waited the entire day for the result of the blood test, and when it finally came we were informed that her blood was perfect, but that it was now too near Easter to put her on the operating list. We were sent home with the promise that we would be summoned again the next week. I thought our treatment throughout the whole episode had been casual and shabby, but I dared not complain. We set out on the long trek back to Hereford to spend Easter with the family. Clare expressed her feelings by standing in the middle of Paddington station and wailing, 'I don't want to have my tonsils out.'

After Easter, since Stephen was free of responsibilities for a while, we agreed to go back to London as a whole family to be with Clare. On the night before she returned to hospital, Stephen and I discussed the situation. Up till this point we had prayed regularly for Clare in the prayer group that we held every week in the Vicarage, but we had found it difficult to pray with her in person, feeling that it was hard to be objective about one so close to us. We knew the time had come for us to remove this barrier, so we went upstairs to the children's room and knelt down beside Clare's bed. While we were happy to accept surgery for the tonsils, we were not too keen on the idea of grommets, so we laid hands on her and began to pray. Suddenly she rolled over and began to snort and snuffle loudly. This was quite normal, as her breathing was restricted by the tonsils which almost met at the back of her throat. After a few seconds I collapsed into helpless laughter and Stephen followed. 'This is like praying over a little piglet,' I said, as Clare continued to snort. We composed ourselves and again laid hands on her, only to collapse in giggles once more after a few seconds. 'This is no good,' Stephen said. 'We must be serious.' I disagreed and said that we were not laughing at what we were doing, but at the piggy noises, and that our prayers were in earnest. So we continued to pray and giggle alternately.

Two days later, in hospital, Clare was wheeled back from the operating theatre and I saw that she had cotton wool in her ears. I was puzzled, because I had every confidence that her ears were now perfect again. Later the registrar came down to the ward to talk to me. He was not the same man as we had seen the previous week and he also seemed puzzled. 'I see from her notes that you must have been expecting grommets in her ears,' he said, 'but I have examined them thoroughly and they are both perfectly clear.'

I found myself giving thanks for the botched events of the previous week and I also decided that God has a sense of humour. The subsequent improvement in Clare's health was remarkable; she grew tall and developed colour in her cheeks. Three weeks after the operation she and Anna were bridesmaids at Margaret's wedding in Essex.

The prayer group which we had started the previous autumn had grown in numbers and was by now well established. Stephen and I decided early on in our new ministry that we should have the support of a prayer group behind us and that, if possible, it should be ecumenical. We gathered a group of people, Anglican and Roman Catholic, and met weekly during term-time. Stephen and I would share our activities with the members of the group; and there would be a certain amount of discussion and sometimes Bible study, before we prayed for those known to us, far or near, who were sick in any way. Over the weeks we developed and matured spiritually both as a group and as individuals, and the meeting became an important part of the week for every one of us.

For some months Beth, the mother of Richard, was a regular member of the group. One week she broke down in tears as she told us all how Richard's experience of healing and her own involvement in the prayer group had resulted in the most remarkable repercussions through the network of relationships in her family. We were sorry to lose her when she and her husband moved from the area, but as she bade us farewell, she told us that although they had been in the village but a short while, they believed they had come here for a reason. Jane also joined us in the prayer group and was able to draw great strength from the fellowship and support she found among us. We in turn drew strength from her example of shining peace in the midst of such sadness and turmoil.

At about this time Stephen and I received a visitor named Alison who had been referred to us by her vicar. She had been asthmatic since childhood and was very reliant upon inhalers and steroid treatment. Alison had recently gone through a conversion experience; she was finding Christianity very exciting and was eager to listen and to learn. Because of her open attitude, we found her remarkably easy to talk to and her quick grasp of ideas was refreshing and presented us with a challenge. She saw and accepted the vision of wholeness with no difficulty, and we offered to pray with her in complete confidence that things were going to happen.

We laid hands on her and began to pray. As so often happens when we pray with a person, I was given a picture in my mind. I saw the figure of Christ sitting on the chair opposite Alison. He had her Ventolin inhaler in his hands and he was tossing it gently up and down and wearing a smile that seemed to say, 'I'll have this, you don't need it any more.' Alison appeared much affected by the prayers and when she was able to speak she told us that she had felt tight bands around her chest break and fall free and the sensation of a cotton wool swab being suddenly removed from her throat.

The next time we heard from Alison, a few weeks later, she told us that her recovery was such that she no longer bothered to travel with her inhaler, which she had previously needed to use at least four times a day. Even more marked was her growing spiritual awareness, but she admitted that her enthusiasm sometimes needed to be kept in perspective.

Alison's physical improvement was steady, but she returned to see us on occasion when a problem or a relationship would overwhelm her and cause her asthma to flare up. She was particularly worried about her long-term, brittle relationship with her mother and asked us to pray with her about this. Again we laid hands on her and again I was given an image. Alison was too. She described how she saw herself reaching across a vast abyss towards her mother. Before she left, I asked her if her mother did any knitting. 'That's all she ever does,' was the reply. The picture I had seen was one of Christ sitting opposite an elderly woman and patiently holding the wool around his hands while she wound it into a ball.

As time passed Alison found herself being drawn towards praying for the sick and would come to visit us to share her excitement and wonder. After several months Stephen enquired about her asthma. 'Oh, that's irrelevant,' she laughed.

Stephen and I were gladdened and encouraged by Alison's continuing progress, but I found myself becoming almost depressive, and my physical condition had still not picked up to the level it had achieved before the outbreak of 'flu. On reflection I realised that since we had begun to pray with others a year previously, my own healing appeared to have come to a full stop. I was also aware that I was pushing myself too far and trying to do more than I was capable of doing. I began to limp again and my increasing tiredness emphasised the pain of the residual joint damage in my body.

During June, Stephen flew to Germany to attend an ecumenical conference. He left me to deal with two broken churchyard mowers in the height of the growing season, a broken church clock, the clerical details of a wedding and a funeral and much else besides. Several months earlier he had accepted an invitation to speak about the Christian healing ministry to a group of Young Wives in a neighbouring parish, but the date fixed coincided with his trip to Germany. With reservations I agreed to do the talk for him and spent the few days beforehand in a state of paralytic nervousness, glad that Stephen's mother was helping to keep the household running smoothly. I need not have been nervous. The audience was most responsive and when I opened my mouth, the words came spontaneously. Many questions were asked and I was touched that a number of people gathered round afterwards to share their own stories and experiences both with me and with each other.

The summer term ended with a leavers' service for the Primary School and I prepared the three classes of recorder players I had been teaching all year to play some pieces for the occasion. Anna also performed. She ended the service by playing her harp and singing 'Now the day is over' to an accompaniment she had worked out for herself. As she plucked the first few notes of her introduction and began to sing the simple but lovely melody, the atmosphere became almost tangible and there was barely a dry eye in church. Several days later an elderly man who had been present at the service died after a long illness, and Stephen visited the widow before the funeral. 'My husband was never much of a Christian,' she told him, 'but when he heard your daughter singing he was deeply moved and I think he had a glimpse of a beauty beyond himself.' Perhaps this was a form of healing, but whatever the interpretation, we like to think that maybe Anna was instrumental in playing him to his rest.

12

Stephen was under contract by the publishers to hand in his manuscript by the end of August, so when the summer holidays arrived the children and I went to stay with Mare in order to leave Stephen in peace for a while to finish his writing.

Mare had for some time been involved in the training of a group of Lay Readers and we agreed that I would speak to them about healing at their next meeting. This proved to be a valuable experience and I found the questions and discussions most stimulating.

When I began to wind down from the pace of term-time, the relaxed atmosphere and the extra time on my hands appeared to be having a detrimental effect upon the way in which I was thinking and feeling. My physical pain was not helped by the fact that I was trying hard to entertain the children on my own, and our frequent outings left me flattened and exhausted.

By this time Stephen and I had prayed with a number of people and seen, in every case, marked changes at all levels, though obviously not without cost on their part. I began to dwell on the fact that not only had I come to a standstill where my own healing was concerned, but that it appeared to be so much easier for other people than it was for me. I tried to persuade myself that through the counselling of others, I was growing in spiritual wealth, but I was not convinced. I decided that I was a fraud and on the surface began to lose interest in the idea of having a healing ministry. Below the surface, however, I was well aware of the fact that if Stephen and I had been chosen for this ministry, we would not be let off lightly and that there would be much hard work in the future. I chose to shut this out of my mind and thought only negative thoughts, particularly remembering the attitudes of other people towards me over the past few years. Once or twice people have wandered in and found me resting or in bed and have cheerfully announced, 'All right for some isn't it?' 'Yes it is all right for some,' I wanted to scream. 'It's all right for the some who can get up in the morning, put their own clothes on and run downstairs to begin a normal pain-free day,' – but good manners have so far suppressed that particular outburst. I also remembered flinging a letter to the floor with mixed hurt and anger, when I read, 'How on earth do you find the time to do so much embroidery? I'm always much too busy.' 'Stupid woman,' I thought. 'Doesn't she realise that the reason I have enough time is because I'm incapable of doing anything else?' Of course it is hard to appreciate the pain and disability of another person and I would never wish my experience on anyone, but I found it increasingly difficult to react to the assumptions of those around me, even within my own family, that because I was vertical and on my hind paws, all was now well again.

These assumptions added to the feeling of isolation that had been developing for some time. During the most serious stage of my illness I had become close to many people, who gave me unlimited and unconditional help and support, but as I began to recover, my insistence that I was being healed was met with polite but firm resistance. I was unable to share what I had begun to consider the most important part of my life and growth.

Towards the end of August, when Stephen had completed his book, we visited Hugh at Southampton General Hospital. This was the first time I had seen my embroideries mounted on the chapel walls, and as the sun streamed down on them obliquely through the tall windows and picked out the gold threads and the textures of the materials, I was struck by their beauty. I looked at them as though for the first time with a detachment that belied any involvement with their creation. To me this was proof of the inspiration that can be given to us at the time of extreme suffering and hopelessness. Hugh told me how he considered the embroideries to have a very real ministry of their own. The sister on the rheumatology ward would sometimes bring her despondent patients down to the chapel, when they complained that their hands were useless and that they would never be able to do anything again. She would show them the hangings and tell them about the cripple who made them, and the patients would return to the ward, encouraged to take on projects, however small, of their own. On one occasion Hugh had gone into the chapel and found a man standing by one of the hangings. On his shoulder he carried his little sick child, and the boy was sitting motionless with his face buried, for comfort, in Mary's soft blue robe. When Hugh told me that he had been approached by someone and asked if he would loan the embroideries to an exhibition, I said emphatically, 'No, they belong here, they are needed here,' and Hugh agreed with me.

As we returned home for the beginning of the new term I was overcome with a sense of dread when I saw the term spread out before me with all my responsibilities and the demands that would be made on me. I crawled sheepishly into school one morning and told the head teacher that I could not possibly cope with teaching the recorder players for a while, at least till after half-term. I then settled into a semi-reclusive existence, doing as little as possible and trying to build up my strength.

Every year during October a service for the celebration of Christian healing is held in Hereford Cathedral. A year previously, Stephen and I had been involved when we joined in the laying-on-of-hands. This year Stephen was asked if he would help organise the service. The plan was that it should be an attempt to involve all the healing prayer groups in the diocese, to give teaching and encouragement as well as to offer ministry. Gibson Pattison, one of the people, whom

Stephen had interviewed for his book, was invited to be the guest preacher. It was also arranged that three couples, comprising both laity and clergy, would minister the laying-on-of-hands. The service began fairly formally but after the sermon, Stephen introduced a guided meditation taken from *Christian Healing Rediscovered* by Roy Lawrence. This 'Ring of Peace' helped to transform the formality of the service into an atmosphere where there was a considerable degree of peace, trust and expectancy. When asked to call out the names of absent people needing prayer, there was no hesitation; the response was immediate. After the meditation, the congregation were invited to come forward for ministry. As the first person knelt down in front of Stephen and me, all my recent feelings of inadequacy and fraud were dispelled by a rush of what I can only describe as tremendous power. As we laid hands on the man, I had to steady myself for fear of falling as the sensation flowed through me and caused temporary dizziness. A large number of people came forward for prayer and as the service progressed, I felt privileged to be taking part.

The following morning I felt stronger at every level and realised that I had been lifted out of the temporary trough I had wallowed in for some months. I wrote a letter to Hugh shortly after this; he had been concerned about me in the summer and I wanted him to know that I was beginning to improve again. He telephoned me on the morning that he received my letter, to tell me of two dreams which he had had about me and which had puzzled him. In the early autumn, at the time of my gloomiest phase, he had seen me, in a dream, sitting in a darkened room, staring at the wall. There were no windows and no door and I was alone. During the week of the cathedral service, he had seen me again in the same room, facing the same wall, but this time there was a door in the wall. It was open slightly, and there was light streaming through it.

The service was talked about for some time afterwards, and gradually reports began to filter through to us of people who claimed to have been healed at the time or since. I was presented with a situation with which I had long wondered how I would cope, should it arise. Stephen came home one day with the news that a man suffering from arthritis had been healed after we had prayed with him. I had always been afraid that if this happened, I might be tempted to feel some resentment, but to my relief my reaction was that of wonder and genuine pleasure on behalf of the man. He later wrote us a letter and told us how he had walked from the cathedral that evening quite free of pain.

As time went on more people began to contact us and ask for our help. One of them, Polly, came, having heard about us through her friend who had been present at a talk that I had given. She was asthmatic, and as well as fighting with the condition from which she has suffered since her early twenties, she was also struggling with an unsatisfactory marriage. Polly told us that since early in her marriage, she had been dominated and repressed by her husband. While raising her children, she was able to tolerate his attitude, particularly as she was also holding down a responsible job, of which she suspected he was jealous. Now in her forties and with children away from home, she was determined to discover her own identity, and was clearly seeking a peace and harmony in her life. She recognised that her asthma attacks were generally being triggered off by the tense atmosphere at home and prolonged by the accompanying impatience and lack of sympathy.

Polly was not seeking marriage guidance, nor was she seeking to change her husband in any way. She wanted to rid herself of the asthma. Up to this point she had never really thought in terms of the spiritual dimension of her problem. Of all the people to whom we talked, however, she grasped most readily the relevance of the ideas that we wanted to share with her. One key concept that we find helpful to explain is that of 'repentance'. This does not involve grovelling confession; rather it directs people to the realisation that they need to find, with the help of God, a new direction for

91

their lives. Repentance also involves letting go of things that are shown to be obstructions in the task of 'living within the will of God'. Sometimes the things of which they have to let go belong to the present; more often they are attitudes and feelings with their roots deep in the past. Polly quickly recognised that when we humbly open ourselves to God's will, then he is able to deal with the problems. Up to this point she had fought her problems with the aid of self-help manuals and intense self-analysis; now she recognised the possibility of relaxing and letting go in prayer and finding that God was in control.

Stephen and I found ourselves challenged initially by having to deal with a person whose assumptions at the start were in no way Christian. But by this stage we were sufficiently confident in the reality of our ministry to be able to present it in terms that she could accept and make her own. We suspect that many church-going people would find unacceptable our insistence that God is concerned to break through into our lives when we let him, but here with Polly who came to us in distress and need, it was once again a case of 'Blessed are they who know their need of God'. Her need enabled her very quickly to realise the reality of which we were speaking. As we laid hands on her head and began to pray with her, I felt again the tremendous sense of peace and power, which I was now experiencing in varying degrees whenever we prayed with the sick. Polly, too, spoke of peace and of a warmth which spread through her whole being.

The next time we saw her was shortly after Christmas. She had sailed through the exhausting activities of a family reunion and she had suffered from 'flu. In spite of this, she had not wheezed once and had even coped with a personal crisis with a degree of calmness that had won the rare respect of her husband. Polly came to see us every month for a while and told us of her increasing ability to override the storms, both at home and at work, with an assurance and inner peace. She was able to view her relationships from a different perspective, and her physical improvement was being maintained. After some months she moved house and we temporarily lost touch, but on her last visit to us she asked us to pray with her. As we did so I had a vision of her climbing a steep hill. I saw Christ standing at the top waiting for her, and when she reached him they walked together along the brow of the hill. I told Polly this, and she was amazed, as she had had a similar vision. 'I was climbing a hill', she said, 'and someone was at the top. I don't know who it was but he was waiting for me.'

13

From time to time Alison would contact us and tell us about
what she was learning and discovering. Shortly after the
cathedral service in the autumn, she had met and formed a
friendship with a woman named Karen, and the two of them
began to pray together. Karen had apparently been at the
service; she had come to Stephen and me for the laying-on-of-
hands and asked for the healing of strained family relationships. Within a month, remarkable changes had taken
place within her family. She had met Alison and the two of
them had felt themselves drawn towards praying for the sick.
Feeling themselves to be diffident and shy, in spite of their
underlying confidence in what was expected of them, they
came together to see us a few times and we were able to
encourage them and offer a sounding board for the ideas and
insights which they were discovering all the time. In talking
to them I remembered the words of Jim Sepulveda on an
occasion that I managed to spend a couple of hours with him
on one of his subsequent visits to England. 'I can teach you
nothing,' he said. 'Be true to yourself so God can work
through you and be himself through you.' He told us that
new insights would be revealed to us by degrees and that we
must always be open and ready to learn. This advice, which
had been so valuable to us, was now in turn offered to them.

All through our growth in the healing ministry Stephen
and I had felt guided and led in such a way that each new
'crisis' was indeed an opportunity for discovery and new
learning. New situations were not met with a sense of
inadequacy, but were welcomed as a chance to learn,
through the Spirit, something new. This openness to the

Spirit was, we felt, far more important than seeking training from professionals, even were such professionals to exist. Once or twice I have been asked whether or not I have had any formal training in counselling. My answer has been that if years of illness and pain have not taught me something of compassionate concern for the sick, then I could never acquire it from professional counselling training.

It is this realisation that my suffering has granted me a capacity for deep identification with the sick, combined with a sense of being led and guided by the Spirit, that has given me the confidence to be involved in this ministry. I hope that this confidence will never lack humility. Perhaps humility can always be preserved as long as we see the ministry as a journey to God's will for our lives, and we never claim that we have arrived! On the face of it, it would appear that to have spent almost half my life being ill one way or another has been a wretched waste of time, but when I consider that I have experienced illness on organic, structural, depressive and psychic levels, in fact everything but terminal, then I see the accumulated experience as a great wealth to be shared with those who need it.

Some time after Stephen and I began our ministry to the sick, I was listening one day to a tape on which a cathedral choir was singing a collection of psalms, among them Psalm 84. As I listened to the words I was struck by the verse: 'Who going through the vale of misery, use it for a well, and the pools are filled with water.' Suddenly I knew exactly what that meant, at least in the context of my own experience. All those years of pain and suffering had not been wasted but rather were collected in a well to be drawn from whenever there was a thirst. This water, although collected over a period of time, was kept continually fresh through prayer and a desire to be led by the Spirit.

Our weekly prayer group became very important to us as a source of constant renewal and encouragement. The trust and the love that developed between the members of the group enabled all of us to share our insights and problems and to gain perspective from one another. The trust that can develop between those who pray together is a greater trust than I have met at any time and I believe it to be a vital force in the strength and efficacy of our prayers for the sick. We received many pleasing reports from people who had been included on our prayer list, and one person in particular should be mentioned. We learned that a woman named Diana, who lived in the village, was suffering from cancer. Stephen visited her several times but the conversation never really deepened beyond the subject of her treatment or the progress of her children. Although she was remembered weekly when the prayer group met, Stephen and I felt unable to approach her and talk about Christian healing. Then one month we decided to attend Peter Scothern's meeting. We had not been at one for a long time, and as we sat down we found ourselves directly in front of Diana and two of her friends. After the meeting she smiled at me briefly and made a hasty exit.

The following Sunday was Mothering Sunday and I noticed that Diana was among the congregation at the children's service. She came up to me and said, 'Pain's gone.' I expressed delight and she added, 'Went during the meeting.' After this positive announcement Stephen decided to go and visit Diana and find out more. It appeared that she had had a definite experience of some kind and that she believed, in a childlike way and unconditionally, that she was being healed. She confidently told a number of people and even persuaded a few to attend the next meeting at the Shire Hall with her. As time passed, she lost her translucent green appearance and continued to affirm her healing. When Stephen reported her progress to the prayer group, we all felt sure that it was continued prayer that had helped send Diana into a situation where she could best be helped.

Every time that Stephen and I prayed either with or for a person, we knew that the prayer would be used, though not how it would be used. We were always as eager and excited to learn of the progress of others as they were to relate it. One criticism that I have heard levelled at those with a healing ministry is that surely psychotherapy could do the job equally well and is it not the skill of the counselling involved that helps a person to recover? I think the following stories could help to answer these questions.

For some time we had been friendly with a woman named Josephine. She had recently been widowed and after overcoming the initial problems of bereavement, she began to worry about her direction both for her future life and on a spiritual level. She often appeared upset and detached but nevertheless showed an active interest in what Stephen and I were doing. 'I don't think I could be helped,' she would say. 'I haven't sunk to the bottom yet.' We would have liked to have offered help long before she reached the bottom, but the initiative had to come from her.

Then one day she did ask for help. She spoke, as always, of her want of direction and her need of an inner peace and as we laid hands on her and prayed, we thought in particular of these problems. Some weeks later I answered the front door to Josephine, who was anxious to share her news with me. 'I did go right to the bottom after you prayed with me,' she told me. 'I needed to get there before I could be pulled up again.' She revealed that for a considerable time she had been slave to a condition called bulaemia, literally ox-hunger, or compulsive eating. She would often eat till she vomited, and knew that she was creating a vicious circle of unhappiness, eating, vomiting and back to unhappiness. She had kept this a secret from her family and felt unable to share it with anyone else, fearing the reaction. Two years earlier she had heard on the radio a programme about people suffering from the same problem and realised that she was not alone. The next week, however, she listened to the same programme and heard some of the letters which had been written in response to the programme on bulaemia. 'How can you give broadcasting time to discussing such revolting people?' asked one of the letter-writers. On hearing this, Josephine was loth to admit, even to herself, that she had the condition. She felt lonely and isolated not only because she was unable to share her problem, but also because her requests through prayer for divine support were apparently not being answered. She felt continually as though she were being thrown back on herself.

By the time Josephine came to see us, she had settled into a 'you're on your own' frame of mind and found it difficult to accept that God had any interest in her. While we prayed with her, I saw a very simple vision, just that of Christ sitting quietly by the head of her bed in a darkened room lit only by a small lamp. She smiled when I told her about it, but with a slight air of disbelief. For two or three days Josephine became progressively more depressed and desolate and then at her lowest point she remembered an advertisement she had frequently seen in slimming magazines: 'Are you a compulsive eater? Ring this number for help.' She had known that a clinic existed to help those suffering like herself but had refused to acknowledge that she needed help; that was for other people. Now in the very depths of despair, she realised that her immediate step forward was to contact the clinic. The voice on the other end of the telephone was reassuring and said, 'You can't shock us, we've heard it all before.' Josephine knew that at last she had found someone who would understand her. Slowly and gradually she became aware that she was not alone and that the quiet figure sitting constantly by her was a reality. Through her contact with the clinic and her growing awareness of God's presence in the situation, she began to increase in both spiritual and personal strength and to work with a greater confidence towards the defeat of the condition which had caused her so much misery.

I feel this to be a fine example of how prayer can be used. Stephen and I had no idea of Josephine's problem, but God knew, and he took our prayers and used them to bring Josephine the help and encouragement she so desperately needed.

Shortly after this we were contacted by a young woman

named Jan. She had recently been diagnosed as having rheumatoid arthritis and wondered if we could help her. A friend of hers had heard me give a talk on one occasion and had told Jan all about it. 'Oh no,' I thought, 'not an arthritic!' I thought of my own long-drawn-out illness and my continuing search for complete healing, and I felt cowardly about being faced with a similar situation. I remembered the man who had received healing at the cathedral service, but then I had not been involved with counselling him.

Jan proved to be an interesting person. She had moved between various Christian traditions and had a mature outlook, but since the diagnosis of her illness she had experienced increasing spiritual dryness. The first few times she came to see us we discussed many things concerned with her personal and spiritual life, and as we talked to her and prayed with her, she seemed to grow in understanding and awareness. But the rheumatoid arthritis became, if anything, gradually worse.

Stephen sensed one day that Jan was not telling us all that she might, and asked if there were any problem or unhappiness that she had not yet mentioned. She then told us, almost casually, that she had had an abortion in her late teens, but that she had recovered from it and now gave it little thought. She seemed a little too emphatic in her insistence that she had got over the trauma involved, but Stephen and I felt it to be important that we pray for the healing of this memory and for Jan to know the forgiveness of the child, and indeed learn to forgive herself. She agreed with less than her usual conviction. I placed my hands on Jan's head and Stephen began to pray and at once I saw in my mind, Christ standing with a baby in his arms and I felt the room fill with a tremendous peace.

I did not feel moved to tell Jan of the vision that I had seen; somehow the time was not right. A few days later she came to see us again and reported that the subject of the abortion had been constantly niggling at her, although it had never done so before. 'Perhaps it is niggling because it needs to be brought out and you need to come to terms with it,' we suggested. Jan spoke of the incident in mechanistic terms and admitted that she had pushed aside the thought of there being another human being involved, to make it easier to suppress the memory. At this point I felt it right to tell her about the picture I had seen of Christ with the baby in his arms. Jan sat very still and stared straight ahead of her with a dazed expression and then suddenly she broke down. 'Oh, what a beautiful picture,' she whispered, and then put her head down and wept.

We next saw Jan after a fortnight. She bounced in and flopped into a chair. 'Is that chair too low for you?' I asked, remembering her former discomfort. 'Of course not,' she beamed. 'I'm better now.' She had gone home after her previous visit and cried for hours and had even discussed everything with her husband. Almost from that moment, she had begun to recover and by the time she was due to see us she was convinced of the healing she had received, to the extent that she planned to visit her doctor and hand back all the drugs he had prescribed for the rheumatoid arthritis. Jan spoke of peace and a great sense of release. By acknowledging the reality of her baby she had been able to hand it into the keeping of God and know that the weight had been lifted from her own shoulders.

This decisive breakthrough might be thought of in terms of a psychotherapeutic release, but for Jan the important thing was not only the tears but the realisation of a forgiving, healing God, who enabled her to face the painful experience in her past. I forgot my earlier reservations of being asked to help an arthritic and I realised that the physical manifestation of a disease was of less relevance than the spiritual and emotional dis-ease which it represented and that I was not to think of people as arthritics, asthmatics or whatever.

As time goes on I feel a growing confidence when I speak to people about healing. I no longer feel that I need the approval of my listener and I realise that there is no one who has the right to deny another person's experience of healing.

To do so would be to challenge their relationship with God and the growing awareness and understanding that is at the heart of every healing experience.

Strangely enough I have found it difficult when talking to some members of both the clergy and the medical profession. There are a minority in both camps who are delighted and even strengthened by what has happened to me, but a number of the clergy appear mildly embarrassed by this evidence of God's power in the context of our daily lives and many doctors think that I am experiencing a natural remission. They cannot accept the idea of a supernatural 'remission'.

Equally strangely it is the reaction of those outside the organised Church which I generally find the most positive and I am greatly encouraged by this. I find it easier in some cases to discuss healing with friends and acquaintances who would probably claim to be agnostic, and I detect a greater openness and willingness both to discuss and to learn than is sometimes found among those of us who have been conditioned and moulded by a formal structure of belief and worship. I find this encouraging, because I believe it indicates a large and untapped potential for the Christian faith. I frequently speak to people who have a wider vision and understanding of an ultimate being than those who give lip service to Christianity. It would appear that belief, whether in a particular form of medical practice or in a God who works in accordance with certain rules, is stronger than a readiness to accept the unexpected. Agnostics, on the other hand, are often better able to take seriously the mystery of healing; perhaps because they have no belief system which is under attack.

Only one person's response has really saddened me. The husband of a good friend wrote and expressed his concern that I had been treated by an acupuncturist. He accused me of messing about with the occult and even suggested the form of prayer I should use to release myself from this evil and the trouble it could cause me in the future. I asked him, courteously, to provide some evidence to support his claims but I have never heard from him or his wife since. It is a sorry situation when intolerance can destroy what I considered to be a strong and lasting friendship.

The question that I have been asked more times than any other is 'Why do you think God has given you this disease? Doesn't it affect your faith?' I answer that I do not believe in a God who hands out suffering, and that such an idea is utterly contradictory to the belief that God wants to heal us. I do believe, however, that God can and does use suffering and I have clear evidence that my own illness has borne unexpected fruit in many directions. So yes, it has affected my faith, it has strengthened it as I witness God's great compassion and desire to heal his people.

14

Exactly two years after we visited Juliet in hospital, she
came to stay with us. Our correspondence had been patchy
and I was not quite sure what to expect. I was amazed. She
waltzed up the steps and in through the front door, moving
with two sticks at a much faster pace than I had yet been able
to achieve. She told me that her consultant was thrilled by
her progress and that in time she would be able to walk
without her sticks. Each time her hips were x-rayed, it was
shown that the cartilage between ball and socket was
gradually regenerating and that in time there would be
sufficient to cushion her weight without the aid of sticks.
Juliet also told us more details about the original operation.
One of the muscles had to be detached and reattached to the
bone during surgery and therefore she would not have been
expected to have much movement in her leg, let alone shoot
it up at right angles after only a month. It was this movement
in particular that had stunned the doctors. Perhaps the
gentle movement that I felt under my hands had been the
muscle tissue healing and strengthening. We shall never
know the answer to that question, but we do know that
Juliet was the only one of several on the ward having similar
surgery, who had both her hips done within a few weeks of
each other. Everyone else had been sent home for a number
of months between operations.

Juliet spoke of the way in which she had grown spiritually
over the past two years, and we found that there were many
parallels not only in our physical progress but also in the
discoveries that we had made and the insights that had been
given to us. It seemed that our joint experiences had brought

us to a common mind. In particular we believed that we were not being healed 'from' something but that we were being healed 'for' something. In my case this was already beginning to take shape and in her case was a discovery to look forward to.

Although I write that things were taking shape, they were by no means static or predictable. Stephen and I learned very early on that we had no control over who came to us or what happened subsequently to each individual, or indeed to ourselves. The realisation that we were not in control began to take from each situation the element which could easily have turned into stress, had we not been able to hand over entirely to God. In a sense we were learning to pass the buck without feeling guilty about it. Sometimes I have attended meetings at which I have heard people being told to 'name it and claim it', with regard to their healing, but I have not been entirely happy with this approach. It would appear that this a subtle form of trying to control God's intentions. There is no doubt that he always uses prayer, but very often in the most unlikely way. This is one of the exciting aspects of praying with the sick; the outcome is so often unexpected. In fact there is never a situation, however hopeless or desperate, from which God cannot raise a person and then create something from the suffering, if he is allowed to do so. This is true even when praying with the dying. If we believe that healing is to do with enabling God's will in every situation and acknowledge that even at the point of death, God's will can still be done, then it is right to offer prayer whenever it is requested. There are countless examples of people who, through prayer, have witnessed in the last days of their lives the healing of attitudes and broken relationships and have died with a greater realisation of the reality of God's presence and peace.

Up to this point I have written about the success stories in our ministry, but the picture has not always been so rosy. To begin with, there is the fact that our ministry has not been readily accepted within our own community and virtually all of those coming to us for help have come from elsewhere. So apart from the tremendous support we continue to receive from the members of our prayer group, we have felt, at times, very isolated in what we are doing. The events of the past few years have obviously changed us, and not all our friends and family have been able to keep up with the change. It is not that we have become in any way fanatical or identified with a 'party' presentation of Christianity; rather that the experiences that we want to communicate go beyond the bounds of what ordinary language can easily convey. Also, as Stephen tries to express in his book, we find ourselves with our sympathies greatly enlarged and able to cross many of the barriers within traditional Christianity. Somehow the experience of healing has brought us to the point where Christianity is simultaneously enormously broad and also very simple. This perspective, which is a point of encounter with the living God, makes many of the issues of church life seem terribly unimportant. The change from a complicated wordy Christianity to one of great simplicity has meant that we find ourselves out of step with many Christians, who seem to prefer their faith expressed in an enormous number of words and concepts. While words are of course important to us we stress the need to leave them behind in some way, if we are to know the reality of a God who forgives and heals through prayer.

It would seem from the literature on healing that is available that many ministries never encounter failure, or at least choose not to write about it. Our experience has been that although prayer is answered in every case, sometimes the individuals for whom prayer is offered erect barriers for themselves, so that little is achieved in the long run. There is a need for people to play their part in the healing process, and it is not difficult for them to resist whatever God wants to do for them. The answer to prayer is of course found not only in physical healing but in any new orientation to God, where his will for a person becomes a reality.

The discovery of this appears to be deeply disturbing for

105

some people. In the case of Jeffrey, a man in his forties, his first visit to us resulted in a significant removal of symptoms of a circulatory problem, a relief which lasted two days. He came to see us a week later and we expected him to show some pleasure at this relief, albeit short-lived, which we interpreted as a 'promise' of more permanent healing. His reaction, however, was pessimistic and we felt a considerable resistance, which had not been evident the previous week. We never saw Jeffrey again; he telephoned us before his next appointment with the words, 'I don't think this is for me.' In our first session we had touched on certain vulnerable areas of his life which seemed to result in the limited measure of healing. When he next visited us, he appeared to become aware of the work that would have to be done to progress further; this he was unwilling to do. Up to this point we had found everyone ready to work at their healing, particularly when, as with Jeffrey, the first time of prayer had given them evidence that God was interested in them and on their side.

There is an irony in the fact that although we are discovering, with God's help, the discernment needed to uncover people's deepest hurts and thereby help them move towards their healing, I seem unable to apply this to myself. I in turn have sought help from others but can discover no indication of why my physical healing slowed down when I began to pray with others. On the other hand I do acknowledge the considerable emotional healing and spiritual growth, which I continue to experience, and I know that I am happier and more balanced than at any other time in my life. Perhaps I must accept, as St Paul did, that God is able to use physical weakness as a vehicle of his power. Also my continuing pain makes it impossible for me to be either over-confident or proud in what we are being led to do. But through the shortcomings of my own healing I occasionally become undermined and lacking in confidence when faced with the responsibility of helping others. Then I find myself in another situation, which I know to be part of the mysterious

106

process through which God is leading us. Once again I feel compassion; a person receives healing and I feel privileged to be part of it.

My story concludes not with a fairy-tale ending, but with an awareness that in all the stages of my life, there has been a pattern in God's care and concern for me. This has not often allowed me to avoid my suffering but it has enabled me to learn in it and through it the precious truth that life begins to make sense when God's will, his Kingdom, begins to break through. Healing, my own and that of others, has made me very much aware of the reality of this will of God at work in the world. Once encountered, this Kingdom of God and Christ who proclaims it, are very hard to deny or escape. This story could well be summed up as being an account of what happens when God breaks through into the life of an individual, but of course, what happens to an individual will always affect the immediate and closest members of the family. Stephen, Anna and Clare have all in their different ways suffered beside me in my illness and all of us have, through my gradual healing, grown together in love and understanding. We look forward to the future in the hope and expectation that God has many more surprises for us.